THE GENIUS OF PAUL

As Moses gave the Law to the Israeli[...] [...] of the Cross to the world. In separati[...] [...]brother of Jesus, he created a new rel[...] ...at was to inherit the empire of pagan Rome and still dominates Western culture today.

In this explanatory translation of Paul's letters, the power of his extraordinary personality and revolutionary message of mystical faith come to life as never before.

SIDNEY BRICHTO is a leading Liberal, Jewish Rabbi and theologian who writes and lectures on religious and moral issues.

Also published in *The People's Bible* series:

Genesis
The Books of Samuel
Song of Songs
St. Luke & The Apostles

The Conquest of Canaan [Joshua and Judges]

The People's Bible

The Genius of Paul

Paul's letters to
the Thessalonians, Corinthians, Galatians,
Romans, Philippians, Ephesians, Colossians,
Philemon, Timothy and Titus

newly translated by Sidney Brichto

Sinclair-Stevenson

First published in Great Britain by
Sinclair-Stevenson
3 South Terrace, London SW7 2TB

British Library Cataloguing in Publication Data
A CIP catalogue record for this book is available from
The British Library.

ISBN 0 953 73985 6

Typeset by Rowland Phototypesetting Ltd, Bury St Edmunds, Suffolk.
Printed and bound by Bookmarque Ltd, Croydon, Surrey.

Dedicated to
EVELYNE BARCLAY
a woman of valour

This series of new interpretative translations has been made in memory of my brother, Chanan Herbert Brichto. He loved the Bible with enormous passion not for its historical veracity but for its moral and literary genius. All the scholarly innovations in my translation are his. His seminal books Towards a Grammar of Biblical Poetics *and* The Names of God *will, I am convinced, in time revolutionize biblical scholarship. His respect, bordering on worship, of those geniuses who were the vehicles of the Still Small Voice of God, is what inspired me to make this attempt to give the Bible back to the people of great, little, or no faith.*

I want to thank Christopher Sinclair-Stevenson whose faith in the project never wavered when my own confidence began to ebb. This attempt is as much his creation as mine. I thank Beverley Taylor, my personal assistant for so many years, for her dedication and help in enabling me to fulfil my creative interests; and to my wife and children for their advice and patience in my pursuit of this ambitious project.

SIDNEY BRICHTO

Contents

The order in which the letters are printed in the traditional Bible is in order of diminishing lengths. The order below is based on an estimated chronological sequence.

Preface

The simple purpose of this new Bible is to give it back to people who welcome a good story, fine poetry, and inspiration. For too long now, the Bible has become the best-seller least read. There are several reasons for this, foremost among them the claim of believers that the Bible was written or inspired by God. As our age has become increasingly secular such a claim has turned people away. Also, atheists and humanists maintain that the Bible is a pack of distortions and false prophecies which prevent men and women from accepting their full responsibility for human destiny.

Literate people, however, aware of the Bible as a great classic, feel obligated to read it. Most do not get very far. Repetitions, lack of chronological order, tedious genealogical inserts, stories which cry out for explanations which are not given, incomprehensible thoughts – all these elements, as well as the formal divisions into chapters and verses, have forced most readers to give up even before they have reached the middle of the first book of Genesis.

The purpose of this edition of the Bible is to recast it in such a manner as to make it readable. It will be the complete biblical text faithfully translated after reference to other translations. The biblical narrative style is so sparse that it leaves much to the imagination. This provides a challenge to consider what the author has left out. On occasion, the translator will respond by interacting with the text to fill out the story. To avoid confusion, such elaborations will be indicated by a different print font. This is done with the expectation that some readers will feel that they (and indeed they may be right) could have done better. Such reactions are welcome and proof that the translator's objective of making the Bible come alive has been achieved. Material which appears irrelevant and interrupts the flow is moved into an appendix. Words and sentences will be added, also in a different print font, when necessary to provide continuity and to remove seeming contradictions. References will abound, to enable the reader to find the place in a traditional Bible should he or she wish to make comparisons.

Since the Bible is a library of books, each book or group of books will therefore require special treatment, with a specific introduction to explain how the translator has dealt with the material in his attempt to enable you not only to possess a Bible but to read it with comprehension and with pleasure.

Introduction

It should not be a surprise if the man who revealed the mystery of the Cross should himself be the most enigmatic of men. His letters are the earliest writings of the New Testament. The Gospels and The Acts of the Apostles were written after the deaths of the apostles. The fact that those who canonised the books of the New Testament were not disturbed by contradictory reports in the Gospels is an indication that their concern was not historical accuracy but conveying the message of Jesus's divine role in the unfolding of man's relationship with God. Paul's letters are therefore the earliest written records we have of the new teachings and reveal his paramount influence in forming Christian theology.

The contents, passion and style of the letters reflect a human dynamo – a man who is running on all cylinders. His audiences would have been mesmerised as he swung from gentle pleadings to fierce attacks on them for not being obedient to his instructions. The mixture of praise and blame, expressions of love and disappointment, must have confused his disciples as much as his opponents. If his sermons were anything like his letters, it is hard to understand how anyone could have fallen asleep while listening to them, as Luke claims happened to a young man hearing him in Troas. He expresses the full panoply of human emotions: hope, despair, a sense of grievance and being misunderstood. He turns from being defensive and apologetic to warnings of the dire consequences of ignoring his exhortations.

Paul is a self-confessed fanatic. The ferocity with which he declared the good news was no less than that with which he had previously hounded the followers of Jesus. Considering his vision of Jesus and his conviction that he was on an urgent mission to save the world before the day of judgement which could come at any moment, is it a wonder that he was a fanatic? He would have viewed anything less as sinful lethargy and a neglect of duty.

The validation of Paul's message through the labyrinth of Scriptural texts can deter the reader who might be blinded by the wood because of the trees. But, once one enters the Jewish Roman mind of Paul, his message of salvation is capable of comprehension. First, it is necessary to see the world through Paul's eyes. He was Jewish, a member of the people chosen by God to keep his laws – the Torah – and to be "light to the nations". When they fully observed his Torah, God would send them a messiah, an anointed king, from the Davidic line to restore the sovereignty of Israel. The Temple in Jerusalem would then be the place to which all nations would stream to hear the word of the LORD. The Nazarite sect hailed Jesus as the messiah and awaited his return to fulfil God's promise to place him as king over Israel. This was unacceptable to Paul, a Jew who took pride in his Roman citizenship and loyalty to the emperor. It is for this reason that he persecuted the Jewish Messianists. He was, after all, a Diaspora Jew who did not wish to be identified with any insurrection against Rome by his co-religionists in Judea and Galilee.

But Paul could not *but* be mesmerised by the faith of the apostles and disciples even while he persecuted them. His conversion, however, to Christ was not a conversion to Petrine Christianity but to one of his own inspiration. It is not to a faith in the future of "Jesus Nazarene King of the Jews [INRI]" as was placed over his cross by the jeering Romans, but in his resurrection from death for the benefit of all humanity. Chapter 15 of I Corinthians reveals the essence of the Pauline faith which was to become the basis of Christianity: "The first man was created from earth – therefore earthly. The final man [Jesus] is created from Heaven . . . As we replicated the earthly man so shall we replicate the image of the heavenly man." "This I tell you brothers, that flesh and blood cannot inherit the Kingdom of God just as decadence cannot inherit perfection. I tell you all a mystery!"

The mystery of the cross was that the Kingdom of Jesus was not an earthly one over Jerusalem or Rome but a heavenly one. On Jesus's *parousia*,[1] the living would join the dead to be judged by God and Christ. Those who believed that, in his death of mortal flesh

---

[1] The Second Coming of Christ.

and sin, they had died; and that, in his resurrection, they had been given a spiritual life free of sin – these would be given eternal life, the others would be condemned. To die to one's old self while still alive and to be reborn a new man in Christ and in the holy community of Christ is indeed a mystery.[1]

As the purpose of this translation is to make it accessible as great literature, and not to be a scholarly study of the origins of Paul's faith, I will not explore how this unique faith came to Paul. Some will say that he was influenced by the mystery cults prevalent during his time. The religious will say that he initially received the truth of the mystery of the cross on the road to Damascus. While any conclusions on this subject are of great interest, we must appreciate that they will be based either on personal faith or intelligent speculation. What is of overriding importance to the reader is comprehension of Paul's unravelling of the mystery of the new faith and the Good News, based on Jewish scriptures which he was bringing to the Gentiles.

It is in this context that his attack on the Torah, and his criticism of the other apostles, including James, the brother of Jesus, can be understood. Their vision was too narrow and restrictive. Their attraction to the old Jewish ways was hindering the universal reconciliation of a united humanity to God through Christ. While Paul says he was the least of the apostles, he considered himself the greatest of them – the one who was given a mandate by Christ himself to gather in not only the Jewish exiles but all the Gentiles.

Because of his Jewish nurturing, even when he argues against obedience to the Torah as the way to "justification" or salvation, he is compelled to prove it from the Torah itself. He employs proof texts with a casuistry more impressive and imaginative than any ancient Talmudist or more recent Jesuit: Salvation can only come through grace – the gift of faith – as proved by the first Jew, Abraham who did not stand at Sinai to receive the Law; nor had

---

[1] It was a mystery to be preferred over the Torah because Jews had been observing its precepts and to no avail. Even physical salvation eluded them as they were living at the mercy of their Roman overlords.

he been circumcised when he was praised as righteous because of his faith! The Torah contained laws for men and women who were incapable of obeying them because of the devils who resided in their decadent flesh. As a catalogue of sins and punishments, the Torah was a daily reminder of the evils inherent in human life. The Torah was a curse because had Adam **not** sinned, it would not have been required. The Torah gave false hopes and illusions that men and women could change themselves by scoring divine points through righteous deeds, so adding self righteousness to their already large burden of sins. Only the transformation of sinful flesh into a divine-life-giving-spirit which emanated from God's grace – faith in Christ – could save humanity from itself. The good news was in essence that humans could become the sons of God and together with him judge even the celestial creatures who had fallen from grace.

The genius of Paul was to combine his knowledge of the Torah and Prophets with his profound understanding of human psychology, to persuade and convert the waverers and to strengthen the faith of the believers. When he told his audiences that their faith in Christ meant that they were fortunate to be among the elected because their very faith was itself a proof of God's grace it must have been a powerful incentive for people to cry out: "I believe, I believe!" That their election was built on the previous election of Israel, whose credibility in the Gentile world was great because of the purity of their faith, added force to his argument. Finally, the knowledge that through faith in Christ, his listeners would conquer death as Jesus had and achieve eternal life even while they yet lived was an offer that one would not easily refuse.

Of course, the reader will come across contradictions but they should appreciate that these reflect the contradictions, the tension, in Paul's character. For example, while he transcends his Judaism, he cannot reject his Jewish roots, for Jesus was born a Jew and he, Paul himself, could not divorce himself from the foundations of his own new faith. So, while the majority of Jews rejected Christ, they still remain as God's elected, indeed it was God's will that they reject his son for, had they not, there would have been no impetus to go out to the Gentiles. Once the latter were converted, the Jews would believe and all humanity would be joined to God.

Paul's reputation for misogyny is an injustice. His greatest friends and supporters were women. Those with extraordinary gifts could prophesy, as part of the holy community. The silence he demands of women in group meetings was in keeping with the prejudice of the times that feminine modesty must be maintained in public places. A woman's voice, like a beautiful head of hair, could stir men to lustful thoughts. Paul says that before God there is no difference in the status of men and women, and the man who does not love his wife cannot love himself.

His aversion to sex is also overstated. In a transition period before Christ's reappearance, his view was that all should focus on the ultimate objective and do everything necessary to get a favoured place. Sex and marriage are diversions and distractions from the main opportunity. Nonetheless, being human: better to marry than to lust after another man's wife. Once married, even if you need time for meditation, the marital bond is a contract which entitles both woman and man to sexual satisfaction. In view of Paul's self-imposed celibacy, his acceptance of sexual need is commendable.

I would ask the reader to read the letters with an open mind. Seek to get into the mind of Paul, as I have tried to do while translating them. As a rabbi, I had to distance myself from my own personal convictions to appreciate the breadth and scope of Paul's personality. Christians may have to do the same, for so many prefer Jesus to Paul. There are those who in their love for Jesus, the man, forget that it is Paul, with all his abrasiveness and arrogance, whose teachings made Jesus the God who has been the centre of Western worship for two millennia. Without Paul there would have been no Christianity. While Christians of a more liberal disposition may not make Paul their role model, they need to acknowledge that if Paul had not succeeded in giving the world the mystery of the death of Christ on the cross the human Jesus could have been forgotten.

A word about my translation. In my version of *St Luke and The*

Apostles, *Christos* was literally translated as "Anointed One" because the drama of his life and death revolved around the expectation that he was a human messiah. In the *Genius of Paul*, I have settled on "Christ" as a fitting description because Paul had transfigured Jesus from a man into the son-of-God, and the use of "Christ" to describe him distinguishes him from the man of earthly flesh perceived by his earlier disciples. *"Ecclesia"* has been translated as "holy community" rather than church, first because it is not an accurate translation and also the modern reader cannot help but think of a building. *Ecclesia* means "congregation" or "community", which is William Tyndale's translation. I have added "holy" because Paul is addressing groups of people who through their faith in Christ have gained the divine spirit and have become part of the body of Christ. I am supported in this because Paul often refers to the believers as "holy" ones. New Testament translators frequently employ the word "saints" which has the same meaning – saint being derived from "sanctus", the Latin for "holy". I prefer "divine" to "holy", because while individuals can make something "holy" by dedicating it to God, that which is of God is already "divine" because it is an emanation of his being. Also, I have used the Latin names to describe the Jewish apostles, rather than the Hebrew names as I did in *Luke and the Apostles* because Paul is working in the Roman rather than the Jewish world.

The Genius of Paul

First Letter to the Thessalonians

F R O M : *Paul, Silvanus and Timothy.*
T O : *The holy community of the Thessalonians in
God the father and the Lord Jesus Christ.*

Grace and peace to you. We always give thanks to God regarding all of you, mentioning you in our prayers and always remembering your works of faith, labours of love and perseverance through hope in our Lord Jesus Christ, in the presence of our God and father. We know brothers, that loved by God, you were elected because our good news came to you not in mere words but with the power of the divine spirit and deep conviction. You know how dedicated we were to you when we were with you. You emulated us and the Lord. In times of severe hardship, you welcomed the message with the joyousness of the divine spirit, and so became an example for all the believers in Macedonia and Achaia. From you, the message of the Lord resounded and not only in Macedonia and Achaia. Your faith in God was known everywhere, so that there was no need for us to say anything. They themselves report how warmly you received us, how you turned to God from the idols – to serve a true and living God; to await the coming of his son from heaven, he whom he raised from the dead – Jesus who is to deliver us from the wrath **of the judgement** to come.

You yourselves know, brothers, that our visit to you was not in vain. Having, as you know, previously suffered and been humiliated in Philippi, inspired by our God we courageously proclaimed the good news to you in the face of great hostility. For our preaching is not the consequence of error, insincerity or deceit. No, God has appointed us to be entrusted with the good news. So we speak not to please men but God who is testing us. You know we never employed words of flattery nor was there any self-seeking motive – God is our witness! We did not seek honour, neither from you nor from others. As apostles of Christ we could have been overbearing but we were gentle with you, like a nurse who cherishes her children. Because we loved you, we were happy not only to share with you the good news from God – but our very souls because you had become so dear to us.

Brothers, you remember our labour and our efforts. We worked night and day not to be a burden on anyone as we preached to you the good news from God. You are witnesses as is God of how our behaviour towards you believers was devoted, fair and faultless. You yourselves know how we behaved towards each one of you as a father to his children – urging and encouraging you and exhorting you to walk in the paths worthy of God who is beckoning you to enter his kingdom of glory.

Also, we never stop thanking God that when you received the word of God, hearing it first from us, you accepted it not as the words of mere humans but truly as the word of God which spiritually empowers you who believe. You, brothers, became like God's holy communities in Judea who are in Jesus Christ, because you suffered at the hands of your own countrymen just as they did at the hands of the Jews,[1] who killed the Lord Jesus and the prophets and also drove us out. They displease God and act against human beings because they are hindering us from speaking to the Gentiles in order to save them. **In so doing** they keep piling up their sins. But God's wrath **and retribution** have at last begun to come upon them.

Brothers, we, bereft of your company for a short time – in the flesh but not in our thoughts – we, because of our longing for you, were desperately eager to see you face-to-face. We wanted to come to you. I, Paul, especially tried to come not only once but twice, but Satan prevented us. For what is our hope and joy and crown of success, if not you, before the presence of the Lord Jesus when he comes. You are **the source of** our glory and joy.

When, therefore, we were exhausted we were happy to be left on our own in Athens. So we sent Timothy, our brother and fellow worker for God in the spreading of the good news of Christ to

[1] The reader should not think that this is a blanket condemnation of all Jews – only of those who saw Jesus and his followers as a threat to their own authority and position as the appointees of the Roman Empire.

strengthen you and encourage you in your faith, so that no one should be distracted by these present afflictions. You yourselves know that we were chosen for this – **to suffer these trials.** Even, when we were with you, we told you that we would be persecuted. So it happened as you know. Therefore, when I felt that I could no longer cope, I sent to learn of the state of your faith **for I was afraid** that the Tempter [Satan] tempted you **away from the truth** and that our labour had all been in vain.

So, now Timothy comes from you with the good news of your faith and love, that you always remember us kindly and long to see us even as we long to see you. Therefore, in our distress and affliction we took comfort through your faith. The life in us wells up because you have stood firmly in the Lord. How can we thank God sufficiently in return for all the joy we feel because of you when we rejoice before our God! Night and day we pray with all our heart to see your faces and be able to strengthen any gaps in your faith.

Now, may our God and father himself and our Lord Jesus direct us on the way to you. May the Lord make your love for each other abound and overflow – and for all people, even as is our love for you. May he instil in you pure and holy hearts in the presence of our God and father when our Lord Jesus comes with all his holy ones.

Finally, brothers, we ask you; we implore you in the Lord Jesus, according to our teachings to live in a way pleasing to God – as in fact you are already doing – do it even more! You know what rules we gave you through the Lord Jesus. God's will is that you should be holy by keeping away from promiscuity, that each of you acquires a wife[1] for himself in a holy and honourable manner, not out of the passion of lust like the Gentiles who do not know God; not to go beyond the limits **of decency** in this matter[2] to defraud his brother. The Lord repays such offences, as we have previously told you and confirmed. God called us not to **lives of** impurity but of

---

[1] Or to look after one's own body: variant texts.

[2] Is this referring to the acquisition of a wife or to all contractual arrangements?

holiness. He who rejects this is not rejecting Man but God who has bestowed upon you his divine spirit.

Now, concerning brotherly love, I need not write to you for you are yourselves taught by God to love one another; and you do indeed act in love towards all the brothers throughout Macedonia. But we urge you, brothers, to do even more. Seek tranquillity, do your own business and work with your own hands as we instructed you, so that your life may win respect from outsiders and so that you will not be dependent upon others.

Brothers, we do not want you to be ignorant about those who are asleep **in the sleep of death**; otherwise you will grieve as do the others who have no hope. For if we believe that Jesus died and rose again, so too will God bring **to life again** with Jesus those who died believing in him. This we tell you by the word of the Lord: we who will still be alive to see the coming of the Lord will not have any precedence over those who died **believing in him**. For the Lord himself – at the commanding call, the cry of God's chief messenger, the blast of the divine trumpet – will descend from heaven and the dead in Christ will be the first to arise. Then we who are still alive will be caught up together with them into the clouds to meet the Lord in the air. So will we remain with the Lord forever. Therefore, comfort and encourage each other with these words.[1]

. . . like a thief in the night

Now, brothers, regarding times and seasons **for the coming of Christ**, we need not write to you, for you yourselves know all too well that the day of the Lord will come like a thief in the night. Whenever people say: **We are living in a time of** peace and security – suddenly **without warning** destruction follows like labour pains to a pregnant woman. And there is no way for them to escape, **for it is too late to make preparations.** But you, brothers, are not in

[1] Paul, who preached the second coming of Christ during his lifetime, needs to reassure those believers who have been recently bereaved of fellow believers whom they loved – that all, dead and alive, will be joined together on the day of Christ's judgement.

darkness so that this **coming** day should shock you as a thief would. You are sons of light – sons of the day.

We are not children of the night or darkness. So, therefore, let us not be asleep **to the dangers** as is the rest **of humanity** but let us be watchful and sober. Those who sleep, sleep during the night and those who get drunk, get drunk at night. But we, belonging to the day, let us always be sober, putting on a breastplate of faith and love, a helmet of the hope of salvation, because God has not given us a fate to suffer his wrath but to be the recipients of salvation through our Lord, Jesus Christ; he who died for us so that we might live together with him, whether we keep watch **during the night** or whether we sleep.

Now, we ask you, brothers, to acknowledge those who are working among you, who lead you into the Lord, and who give you counsel. Give them your utmost regard and love because of their work **on your behalf**. Be at peace among yourselves. We exhort you brothers to warn the idle, to encourage the faint-hearted, to support the weak and to be patient and gentle with all people. See that no one returns wrong for wrong but always seek each other's good – and that of all people. Rejoice always, pray continually, give thanks for everything, for this is God's will for you in Jesus Christ.

Do not quench **the fire of** the spirit; do not despise prophecies; test everything; to the good, hold fast; keep away from all evil. May the God of peace, himself, grant you his fullest sanctity so that all of you – spirit, soul and body – will remain faultless before the coming of our Lord Jesus Christ. The one who calls you is faithful. He will achieve it. Brothers, pray also for us. Greet all the brothers with a holy kiss. I charge you by the Lord to read this letter to all the brothers. The grace of our Lord Jesus Christ be with you.[1]

[1] There is growing doubt that the second letter to the Thessalonians was dictated by Paul. My own view is that it is somewhat out of character with his other teachings, especially on the pre-conditions of the second coming. There are some themes from the first letter which are repeated. I have placed the second letter in the Appendix, along with the letter of Timothy and Titus whose Pauline origins I also Question. In doing so, I am making no judgement on its spiritual value – only on its Pauline origins.

First Letter to the Corinthians

FROM: *Paul, by God's will, an appointed apostle of Jesus Christ and Sosthenes[1] our brother.*
TO: *Those who have been made holy through Jesus Christ, known as holy men, the holy community of God in Corinth. All those who in every place who invoke the name of our Lord Jesus Christ – their Lord and ours: Grace and peace be upon you from God our father and the Lord Jesus Christ.*

I always thank God because of the grace of God you have received through **your faith in** Jesus Christ. Through him you have been enriched in all things – in all your eloquence and knowledge, as the testimony of Christ was confirmed by you. Therefore, you lack no spiritual gifts as you await our Lord Jesus Christ to be revealed to us. He will keep you firm **in faith** until the end so that you will be without fault on the day of our Lord Jesus Christ **when he** reappears **to usher in the Kingdom of God and judge both the righteous and sinners.** The God who called you to be partners with his son Jesus Christ is faithful **and will keep his promises to you.** I appeal to you, brothers, in the name of our Lord Jesus Christ that you all agree with each other without differences between you – that you be united with the same mind and purpose. My brothers, I was told by some of Chloe's[2] people that there were quarrels between you. This is to what I refer. One of you says, "I am in Paul's camp." Another says: "I am in Apollos's."[3] Another: "I am in Peter's." Still another, "I am in Christ's." **But I ask you,** is Christ

---

[1] We do not know who Sosthenes is nor why Paul associates him with himself as the sender of the letter. A Sosthenes appears in Acts 18:17 as the head of the Synagogue in Corinth. It is unlikely that he is the same man.

[2] Lest readers think that they have missed out somewhere, I can assure them that this is the only time that Chloe is mentioned.

[3] See Acts 18:24-28. Apollos is described as a powerful preacher from Alexandria who believed in Jesus but as one having a more limited comprehension of the divine nature of Christ.

divided? Paul was not crucified for you, nor were you baptised in the name of Paul. I am thankful I did not baptise any of you except Crispus [Acts 18:8] and Gaius lest anyone should say that in my name were you baptised. True, I also baptised the family of Stephanus, but besides these I do not believe I baptised any others. **I asked others to baptise because I did not want people to feel that my baptisms were better than those of others, for we are being baptised in Christ and it is through him that we receive the grace of the divine spirit and not through he who baptises.**

Christ sent me not to baptise but to teach the good news – not with the human eloquence of brilliant rhetoric, lest the suffering **of Jesus on the** cross lose its significance. For the message of the cross is nonsense to those who are perishing **through their stupidity,** but for us who are being saved it is **the revelation of** God's power. **The disbelievers say if Jesus was Christ – the Messiah – why could he not save himself but we say that he died to save us and in his resurrection restored us to life.**

It is written, "I will destroy the wisdom of the wise. The understanding of the intelligent I will bring to nothing."[1] Where are the sages, where are the scholars and where are the debaters of our age? Has not God revealed that the wisdom of the world is foolishness? The world in its wisdom did not know the wisdom of God. So God preferred **what the world considered** the foolishness of the good news to save those who believed. As Jews ask for miraculous signs and Hellenists ask for philosophical understanding, we nonetheless proclaim that the Messiah was crucified – on the one hand an offence to the Jews and on the other folly to the Gentiles.[2] But to those who have been chosen – both Jews and Hellenists – Christ is both the power and wisdom of God. God's foolishness is wiser than human wisdom and God's weakness is stronger than human strength.

Brothers, consider what you were when you were chosen. Not

[1] Not an exact quotation of Isaiah 29:14.

[2] An offence to the Jews, because while they believed in resurrection of the dead, they expected the Messiah to restore the sovereignty of Israel without first being crucified; folly to the Gentiles because the latter did not believe in resurrection.

many were wise by any human standard, not many were powerful or aristocratic. But God chose foolish creatures to shame the sages. He chose the weak to shame the powerful. But God chose the ordinary and those who were despised – "non-beings" – to reduce to nothing those who are some-bodies, so that no human being should be arrogant before God. It is because of him – God – that you are in Jesus Christ who has become for us God's wisdom as well as our righteousness, holiness and redemption, as it is written, "Let him who boasts boast in the LORD" [Jeremiah 9:24].

When I came to stay with you, brothers, it was not because of my unique eloquence or even wisdom that I declared to you the mystery of God. For I had decided that my only message to you was of **the mystery of** Jesus – **God's** anointed one – and **the fact of** his crucifixion. When I was with you, I was weak through anxiety and in great trepidation. My speech and message ware not proven by the persuasive power of wise utterances but through the demonstration of spiritual strength so that your faith was not dependant on human wisdom but on God's power.

That does not mean that we do not teach wisdom to the sophisticated, but it is not a secular wisdom nor the wisdom of contemporary rulers who are destined to pass away. Now, we are imparting divine wisdom which has been kept secret and hidden away but which God prepared to be for our glory even before the beginning of time. None of the rulers of our time knew this wisdom, for if they had known, they would not have crucified our glorious Lord. But it is as has been written, "That which the eye had not seen, and the ear had not heard and the human mind had not conceived – what God had prepared for those who loved him."[1] But God has revealed it, **his divine mystery,** to us through his spirit.

The **divine** spirit within us explores all things, even the deepest knowledge of God. For who can understand the depths of man except the human spirit. Equally, who could comprehend the thoughts of God except through the divine spirit? It is not the worldly spirit that we have received but it is the divine spirit that

[1] Inspired by Isaiah 64:4

we may comprehend the gift that God has willingly given us. So, we speak of things not taught through human wisdom but with words taught us by the **divine** spirit – interpreting spiritual truths to those who are full of the divine spirit. But the worldly man cannot accept the truths of the divine spirit and considers them as foolish for he cannot comprehend them because they can only be spiritually understood **by those who have been given the gift of the divine spirit.** A spiritual person is able to judge the value of everything, but he himself, **and his own values,** are not to be judged by other people. **As it is written,** "For who has known the mind of the LORD that he should instruct him." [Isaiah 40:13] But we are of those who possess the mind of Christ.[1]

Brothers, **however, I must confess,** I cannot speak to you as men with the divine spirit but as worldly beings – **at best** infants in Christ. I gave you milk as **appropriate for infants,** not solid food, for you were not ready for it. You are still not ready; you still belong to this world. There is jealousy and strife among you – therefore, are you not being worldly? Do you not behave as mere humans **and not as those filled with the spirit of Christ.** For whenever one says, "I follow Paul" or "I follow Apollos" – is that not the speech of men? Who is Apollos and who is Paul? Only servants, through whom you came to believe – as the Lord apportioned **you** to us **both.** I planted. Apollos watered it, but only God makes it grow. Neither he who plants nor he who waters is of any consequence if not for God who makes it grow. The one who does the planting and the one who does the watering are equal and each will receive his reward according to the task he has fulfilled. But we are fellow workers with God. You are God's field, God's building.

I laid the foundation

By the grace of God granted to me, as an expert master builder, I laid the foundation. But another builds on the foundation. But let

[1] An indication that Paul believed that those who believed in Christ could understand the secret thoughts of God. Paul is veritably saying that full Christians have become one with God through Jesus.

each one who builds on it do so with caution. No one, however, is permitted to lay another foundation stone beside that which has already been laid – which is Jesus Christ! Whoever builds on the foundation with either gold, silver and precious stones or wood, grass and straw, his work will be revealed by the light of day. The quality of each man's work will be tested by fire. If what he has built remains intact, he will receive his reward. If what he has built is consumed, he will suffer the loss.[1] He himself, however, will be saved, but only as one who has escaped through the flames.

Are you not aware that you are God's temple and that the spirit of God dwells in you? So that, if anyone destroys the temple of God, God will destroy him. God's temple is holy. You are that temple.

Do not let yourself be deceived. If anyone considers himself as wise in comparison with his contemporaries, let him rather become a "fool" in order to grow wise. For all worldly wisdom, **however impressive it may appear,** is foolishness to God. As it is written, "He ensnares the wise in their own craftiness" [Job 5:13]. Also, "The Lord knows that the philosophy of the wise are futile [based on Psalm 94:11]. So no longer boast about men **and their wisdom.** All is yours! Whether through **the teachings of** Paul or Apollos or Peter – the world, life and death, the present and future – all are yours, for you are of Christ and Christ is of God.[2]

People should regard us as the servants of Christ and guardians of the mysteries of God. Moreover it is required of guardians that they be found to be faithful. For me it is of no matter that I am judged by you or by any human court; I do not even judge myself. I know nothing against myself, but that does not mean that I am innocent – for it is the Lord **alone** who judges me. So judge nothing until the appointed time, until the Lord comes who will shed light on that which is hidden by darkness and will reveal the motives of

[1] The test of Paul's or Apollos's success will be whether or not the believers whom they have inspired will remain faithful to Christ when they are persecuted for their beliefs.

[2] Paul is intoxicated by Christ and seeks to inspire the Corinthians to dismiss whatever doctrinal differences there may be between the different teachings – but to take hold of the mystery of becoming divine through Christ.

our hearts. At that time, each will receive his blessing from God.[1]

Now, I have applied all this – **what I have said** – to myself and Apollos for your sake that you may learn from us to live according to what has been written, and not to go beyond it, **lest with the pretence of greater knowledge** you puff yourself up one against the other. For who is it that distinguishes you from another; and what **knowledge** do you have which you have not received? And, since you have received it **from us**, why do you puff yourself up as though you had not – **that it was your own invention?**

You are full **of yourselves**. You are rich, you rule as kings without us! How excellent it would be if you had become kings so that we might share the kingdom with you,[2] **for though we are apostles it has not been given to us to rule in the Lord's name.** Indeed, I think that God has put us, the apostles, last as designated for execution. We have become a spectacle of derision for the world – to humans and divine beings. We are perceived as fools because we work for Christ, but you – you so wise in Christ! **Ha**, we are weak but you are strong; you are respected but we are despised. Up to now, we are hungry, thirsty, naked, buffeted and without a safe haven. We labour with our own hands – though we are reviled we still offer blessings, though persecuted, we endure. When we are slandered we implore **understanding**. We are considered as the filth of the world and the scum of all things even to this day.

I write this to you not to embarrass you but as admonitions one sends to beloved children. You may have ten thousand teachers in Christ, but you cannot have that many fathers. For in Jesus Christ I have sired you by bringing you the good news. I urge you therefore to follow my example. For this very reason, I send Timothy to you, my beloved child and one who is faithful in the Lord. He will remind you of how I live in Jesus Christ which is consistent with what I preach in every holy community. Because I did not come, some of you became arrogant **and rebellious.** But, the Lord willing,

[1] A wonderfully persuasive self-defence: "How can you judge me when I cannot even judge myself? In the end God will judge.'

[2] What sarcasm!

I will visit you soon and learn not only what these arrogant people are saying, but also what is the extent of their **divine** power for the Kingdom of God is not in words but in **divine** power. What would you like, that I come to you with a punishing rod or with a loving and humble spirit?

It is truly rumoured that sexual licentiousness rages among you and of a kind of which even the Gentiles are not guilty. A man takes to bed his father's wife[1] and you boast of it! Should you not have gone into mourning and removed from your community the man who performed such an act? Even though I am absent in body, I am with you in spirit. And I have already passed judgement on the perpetrator of this deed, as if I had been present. When you assemble in the name of the Lord Jesus and my being is with you in spirit as is the power of our Lord Jesus, hand this person over to Satan to destroy his body in order to save his soul in the day of the Lord**'s judgement.**

Your complacency **over the evil done among you** is not good. Do you not know that a little yeast leavens all the dough? Purge the old yeast that you may become a new loaf, without leavening – for Christ, our paschal lamb, has been sacrificed. **On the festival of Passover we eat unleavened bread with the paschal lamb.** So, let us not keep the festival with old leaven[2] – not with the leavening of malice and wickedness but with the unleavened bread of sincerity and truth. I instructed you in my letter not to befriend the sexually licentious – by which I do not mean that you should not have contact with outsiders who are sexually immoral or envious or ruthless or idolaters – because that would exclude you from the real world. What I am writing is not to befriend anyone who calls himself brother **in Christ** who is licentious, envious, an idolater, a slanderer, a drunkard or a crook. With such a man you should not

[1] "Father's wife" suggests that she is a stepmother. Even so, it is hard to comprehend this type of promiscuity in a holy community. Is it because the Christians lived in a commune – but their seeming approval indicates more: perhaps a misunderstanding of Paul's abrogation of the law, or the belief that repentance through Christ is easy. Messianic sects are often reported to indulge in sexual licentiousness.

[2] Leaven is identified with impurity and sin. I comment on this later.

share a communal meal. What right have I to condemn those outside the community? Must you not condemn those who are within? It is for God to judge the outsiders. But you expel the wicked one from among you!

If one of you has a claim to make against another, how dare you take the matter to law before a pagan court rather than before the holy ones. Do you not know that the holy ones will **in time** judge the world. And if you are to judge the world **by the side of Christ**, are you not competent to give judgement on matters of little consequence? Do you not know that we will be judging heavenly creatures[1]; all the more matters of this human life? Therefore, if you have disputes between you, appoint as your judges even those who are held in little regard. This I say to shame you. Are you claiming that there is not one among you wise enough to judge between his brothers, so that one brother seeks judgement against another brother – and this before non-believers!

And, indeed, is this not a great failure that you have law suits against each other? **According to the teaching of Lord Jesus,** is it not better to be wronged and better to be cheated. But you are the wrong-doers and the cheats – and you do this to your own brothers. Or do you still not know that the wicked will not inherit the Kingdom of God? Do not be deceived. Neither lechers, idolaters, adulterers, gigolos, sodomites[2], thieves, the rapacious, drunkards, slanderers, crooks will inherit the Kingdom of God. And that is what some of you were. But you were washed clean. You became holy. You were made righteous in the name of the Lord Jesus Christ and by the spirit of God.

Your bodies have become part of Christ

While everything is permitted to me, not everything is good for me. While everything is permitted to me, I will not allow myself to be

---

[1] An incredible claim by Paul! Does he mean Satan and the fallen angels?

[2] I would submit that the homophobia of the Old and New Testaments is directed not against "natural" homosexuals (admittedly a modern concept) but against jaded heterosexuals who indulged in all types of decadent behaviour.

ruled by any **hunger or passion.** Food goes into the belly and the belly is there to receive the food, but **in the end** God destroys them both. The body was not intended for fornication. It is for the LORD and the LORD is for the body. Through his power, God raised the Lord **from the dead** and will also raise us. Do you not understand that **through your baptism in Christ** your bodies have become part of **the body of** Christ! How can I then take part of **the body of** Christ and unite it to the body of a whore! Never! Do you not understand that he who joins himself to a whore's body becomes one body with her, for it is written: "The two will become one flesh." But the one who is joined to the Lord becomes one with him in spirit.

Flee from sexual promiscuity. The sins that men commit they do outside the body, **that is against others,** but to be promiscuous is to sin against your own body. Do you not understand that your body is a shrine for the divine spirit which is in you and which you have received from God. You no longer belong to yourself. You have been bought and paid for **through the sacrifice of Jesus Christ.** Use your body then to honour God.

Now, as to matters about which you wrote; it is better for a man not to marry. But, rather than sexual promiscuity, let each man have a wife and each woman a husband. Once married let each perform their marital duties to each other. The wife no longer has sole authority over her body – it also belongs to her husband. Likewise, the husband no longer has sole authority over his body – it also belongs to his wife. Do not, therefore, deprive each other **of sexual contact** except by mutual agreement, and this only for a set period, in order to have the leisure for prayer. But join together again, otherwise Satan will tempt you because of your lack of self-control. **Both you and she will become adulterers if you deprive yourselves of fornication.**[1]

I say this as a concession **to the lusts of the body** but not as a directive. I would prefer it if all men could be like me, but **not all**

---

[1] Paul, like the Pharisees, had a deep respect for the powers of the libido. While celibate himself, his broad-mindedness is indicated by his discouragement of sexual abstinence between a married couple, for that would defeat the purpose of marriage.

have the same dedication that I have. But each man has his own gift from God, **in which he excels.** One has been given this gift while another that gift. **Let none of us become judges over others because of their sexual needs.** So, to the unmarried and widows, I would say it is better to remain unmarried as do I. But, if they cannot control their sexual desires, let them marry, for it is better to marry than to burn **with the lust which leads to sin.** To the married I give the command (in fact it is not mine but the Lord's command) that a woman should not leave her husband, but if she does, let her remain unmarried unless she be reconciled to her husband. Also, a husband must not divorce his wife.

On the other matter, I and not the Lord[1] say this: if a member of the community has a non-believing wife but one who is happy to live with him, he should not leave her. Likewise, a woman who has a non-believing husband who is happy to live with her, she should not leave her husband. For the non-believing husband has been joined to the holy ones[2] through his wife as the non-believing wife has been joined to the holy ones through her husband. Otherwise, **if you did separate from each other**, your children would become impure, but now, **by your remaining together,** they become holy **among those who have been sanctified through Christ.** However, if the non-believer wishes to leave, let him do so. The believing man or woman is not tied in such circumstances. **Do not quarrel with them**, for God has asked us to live in peace. And how do you know, O woman, that you could save your husband or you, O man, that you could save your wife **by persuading them to follow Christ?**

Generally, I would say, each person should be reconciled to the situation in life which the LORD has allotted him. **Because of this view** these are the instructions I give to all the communities. If a man was circumcised when he received the call **from Christ**, he should not hide the marks of circumcision. If a man was uncircumcised when he was called, let him remain uncircumcised. Whether one is circumcised or uncircumcised is irrelevant. What

[1] The humility Paul shows here is quite impressive and to be compared favourably with those clergymen who claim divine authority for their own interpretation.
[2] The literal text is: "has been sanctified."

is important is the keeping of God's commandments.[1] Let every person be reconciled to his role at the time of his calling. Were you a slave when you were called? Do not let your inferior situation worry you. Of course, if you can gain freedom, do so. For he who was a slave when he was called is still a free man before the LORD. By the same token, he who was a free man when he was called became the slave of Christ. You were bought at a price – **the sacrifice of Christ so that you would be saved.** Do not therefore become slaves of men. Each one of you brothers should be satisfied with the situation you were in when God called you.

As to the mater of celibacy, I have no inspiration from the LORD, but my view should have the credibility of one whom the LORD in his graciousness found trustworthy. Because of the present stress **upon us when we await our Lord's return and the beginning of the Kingdom of God, I would recommend,** let a person not change his present status. Are you tied to a woman? Then, do not seek a divorce. If you are a divorcee, do not seek another wife. If you do marry, you have not sinned; and if a virgin marries, she has not sinned. I only want to spare you the hardships **that come as a consequence of marriage.**

This, brother, is my meaning; the time **until the end** is short.

Let those with wives live as though they had none.

Let those who mourn live as though they had nothing to mourn about.

Let those who rejoice do so as if there was no reason to rejoice.

Let those who purchase do so without the feeling of ownership.

Let those who are involved in worldly matters realise the futility of their work.

For the world in its present form is passing away.

I want you to be without anxiety. The single person can dedicate himself to what is important to the LORD and to how he can please the LORD. But the married man suffers the cares of the world – how he can please his wife – and so is divided in himself. The

[1] But circumcision was one of God's essential commandments. What Paul is saying is that what is essential is obedience to the ethical commandments.

unattached woman or the virgin can devote herself to what is important to the LORD. Her desire is to dedicate herself to the LORD both in body and in spirit. But a married woman suffers the cares of the world – how she can please her husband. I say this in your own interest and not to restrict you – but so that you can live properly and wait on the LORD without any distraction.

If anyone is engaged to a virgin, and he thinks he is behaving badly because he has not married her and she is losing the bloom of youth – he should marry her if he thinks that is what he ought to do. In doing this he would not be sinning. Indeed, they should get married.[1] But if a man has made up his mind and there is no pressure upon him and he, having authority over his own actions, has decided not to marry the woman, he also has acted properly. **What I am saying is that** he that marries the virgin has behaved well, but he that does not marry her has even done better.[2] Also, a woman is tied to her husband as long as he lives. If her husband dies, she is free to marry whomever she wants, but only a believer in the Lord. In my view, however, she will be happier if she remains unmarried. However, **in saying this,** I think it is with divine inspiration.

Now, with regard to **believers participating in** meals which have been offered to idols. We know that we all have the knowledge **that these idols are not gods nor do they represent gods and that when we join in feasts with our pagan neighbours we are not worshipping the idols.** But remember our knowledge puffs us up with conceit while love builds up our stature. A man who believes he knows does not know all he should know, but the man who loves God is accepted by God.

Now, about eating idolatrous sacrificial meat, we know that idols have no value in the world and that there is only one God.

[1] Paul shows a sensitivity to the problems of the faithful during the interim period when the followers of Jesus are waiting for the time of judgement. An engaged man should not disappoint a woman because the time was coming when marriage would appear as an irrelevance and when one should concentrate on preparing for the Second Coming of Christ.

[2] But only in the perspective of man being able to dedicate himself to doing the Lord's will.

Even if there are these so-called gods in heaven and earth – and there are many gods and lords – yet, for us, there is just one God, the father, who is the source of all beings and we are in him; also, one Lord, Jesus Christ, who is the source of all beings and through whom we exist. But not all men have knowledge of this. They have become so accustomed to idolatry, that they eat it as meat offered to an idol and so, because of their weak will, they are defiled **through eating it.** But what we eat does not commend us to God. We are not inferior by not eating nor do we excel by eating. But take care, lest you with your authority become a stumbling block for those who are weak willed. For, if someone sees you who "has knowledge" sitting in an idol's temple, will not he be encouraged to eat the meat of idolatrous sacrifices. So, your weak willed brother **in Christ** for whom Christ died is destroyed through **the reputation of** your knowledge. In sinning against your brothers who are so mentally vulnerable, you also sin against Christ. Therefore, if what I eat causes my brother to offend **the Lord,** I will never eat meat again rather than cause my brother to sin.

Am I not a free man? Am I not an apostle? Have I not seen our Lord Jesus?[1] Are you not the result of my labour in the Lord? Even if I am not an apostle for others, certainly I am for you. You are the seal, **the proof,** of my apostleship in the Lord. For those who judge me – this is my defence. Have we not the right to eat and drink? Have we not also the right to the companionship of a believing wife as have the other apostles, like the brothers of the Lord and Peter?[2] Or is it only I and Barnabas who must not stop working **while we minister to you in Christ?**

What soldiers ever work at their own expense? Who plant vineyards without benefiting from their fruits? Who shepherds a flock and refrains from drinking the milk **of its ewes?** This is not merely a

[1] This might suggest that Paul did see Jesus in the flesh, as A N Wilson forcefully maintains [The Mind of Paul – Sinclair-Stevenson – 1997]. I do not think so: Paul is referring to his vision on the road to Damascus.

[2] Paul is here, in my view, boasting of greater dedication to spreading the good news than that of Peter or James. They lead "normal" lives while he crosses the earth to teach Christ.

human view I am expressing. Does not the Torah of Moses say, "You shall not muzzle an ox when it is treading out the grain." [Deuteronomy 25:2] Is God concerned about oxen? He is saying this in relationship to us, is he not? Yes, this was written for us, because when a ploughman ploughs and a thresher threshes, it must be with the hope of partaking **in the harvest.** If we sow spiritual things for you, is it too much to expect to reap material benefit? If others of you in authority are given a share, are we not even more entitled?

Yet, we have not used this right. Rather, we put up with every deprivation so that there should be no obstacle to the good news of Christ. You do know that those who look after the sacred things of the temple eat from its income and that those who minister at the altar eat of the sacrificial food? So did the Lord ordain that those who proclaimed the good news should likewise be supported for teaching the gospel. But I have not taken advantage of any of these rights. Nor have I written this in the hope that I might have such benefits. I would rather die than not to be able to boast of this – **that I receive nothing for ministering to you.** But, of course, I have no time to boast while I am preaching the good news which I am compelled to do. Woe to me if I do not preach the good tidings. If I preach voluntarily, that is my reward, and if under compulsion, that is because I have been entrusted with this stewardship. What then is my reward? It is that in preaching the good news I can do so without charge – not taking full advantage of my rights for preaching the good news.

To all men I become all things

Though a free man without a master, I make myself a slave to all men in order to gain more souls. To the Jews, I am a Jew in order that I might win over the Jews; to those who accept the Torah, while I do not feel bound by the Torah, I become one who accepts the Torah in order that I might win over those who observe the Torah; to those without the Torah I am also without the Torah (but not free of the obligation to keep God's law – that is the law of

Christ) to win over those who do not observe the Torah; to the weak, I became weak to win over the weak; to all men I become all things, so that through every possible means, I might save some. I do this **not for my sake, but** for the sake of the good news that I may share it with others.[1]

Do you not know that, while all run in a race, only one receives a prize? So, run in order to win the prize. Everyone who enters the games goes into training to discipline himself. They do it to win a garland which will wither, but ours will not decay. I do not run without a clear goal, nor do I box against the shadows, but I am severe in disciplining my body and command it as a slave, so that after I have proclaimed **the good news** to others, I should not myself be disqualified **for the prize.**

Brothers, you should know that our forefathers were all under the cloud **in the wilderness** and that they all passed through the **Red** Sea. By the cloud and by the sea they were baptised into **the redemption of** Moses. They all ate and drank of the same spiritual food and drink. **The rock gushed water at the command of God.** But they also drank from the spiritual rock that followed them, which was Christ.[2] God, however, was not pleased with them and their bones were strewn over the desert.[3] Now, these things are warnings for us to keep us from lusting after evil things as they did. Do not be idolaters as some of them were, as it is written, **"Early next morning, they sacrificed burnt and peace offerings [before the golden calf]**. The people then sat down to eat **the sacrificial meal** and drink and got up to play [Exodus 32:6]." Neither should we be sexually licentious as were some of them – indeed in one day twenty-three thousand of them died **for this sin** [Numbers 25]. Nor

[1] Paul is not ashamed of his opportunism because it is for the sake of Christ and not in his own personal interest.

[2] Water springs from a rock [Numbers 20:8] to slake the thirst of the Israelites. According to Rabbinic tradition, a well, in the form of a rock rolled along with them to provide them with water. "Rock" is often used as a description of God because of its reliability, unchanging and supportive qualities.

[3] Because the Israelites lacked faith in their ability to conquer the Canaanites, God decides that the adult generation who left Egypt should die in the wilderness and a new generation should enter the Promised Land. [Numbers chapters 13 and 14]

let us test the LORD's patience as did some of them who were killed by serpents [Numbers 21:6]. And do not grumble and complain as some of them did who were killed by the Destroyer [Numbers 17:14].

Now these punishments were dealt out to those men as examples **of sins we should avoid** and were recorded as warnings to us for whom the end of days is approaching. So let those who think they stand on firm **moral** ground be careful that they do not fall. The temptation you have suffered is not beyond that which is natural to humans. But God is faithful, he will not allow you to be tempted beyond that which you can resist; he will provide you with the means to withstand it.

Therefore, my beloved friends, flee from idolatry. I speak to prudent men: carefully judge my advice. Is not the wine-filled cup with which we praise God a sharing in the blood of Christ?[1] And is not the bread we break a sharing in the body of Christ? As the loaf of bread is one, though we are many, we are one body for we all share in the one loaf of bread. See what the people of Israel do. Do not those who eat the sacrifice share **with their fellows** by the altar **in communion with God? So do we. When I advise you against participating in a pagan sacrificial feast,** am I suggesting that a sacrifice offered to an idol has any significance or that an idol has a value? No, but **still** they are sacrificing to demons and not to God; and I do not want you to be in the fellowship **of those who worship** demons. You cannot drink out of the Lord's cup and also out of the cup of demons. You cannot share both in the Lord's table and in the table of demons. Are we trying to make the Lord jealous? Are we stronger than he **that we can afford to do this?**

Everything which is permissible may not be beneficial, and everything which is permissible may not be fulfilling. Do not seek

---

[1] This symbolism would have been unacceptable to Jews, for they were forbidden to eat any meat which still contained any blood in it. Traditional Jews salt the meat after it is purchased for sufficient time to draw out the remaining traces of blood. In the light of this abhorrence of drinking blood, the blood libel against the Jews that they drank the blood of Christian children on Passover had to be, and was known to be by the Christian Church, an impossibility.

your own welfare but the welfare of others. You may eat anything sold in the meat market without examining your conscience for "the earth is the Lord's and everything in it" [Psalm 24:1]. And if some non-believer invites you home and you want to go, you may eat whatever is set before you without the need to examine your conscience. But if someone says to you, "This has been slain as a sacrifice," do not eat it out of concern for the person who told you, for the sake of conscience – not your own conscience but the other person's. **He is telling you this to see whether you would eat it so that, if you did, he in good conscience could do the same. Therefore I say do not eat of it.**

I will not let my freedom of practices be determined by another man's conscience. And if I participate in a meal with gratitude, why should I be badly spoken about for doing for what I give thanks **to God.** So, whether you eat or drink or whatever you do, do it for the glory of God. Never be a cause for offence, either to Jews, Greeks or the holy community of God – just as I try to please everyone, not to win popularity for my own advantage but for many others that they may be saved.

Imitate me as I imitate Christ. I praise you for always keeping me in mind and for holding fast to those traditions just as I have passed them on to you. The head of every man is Christ and the head of every woman is man and the head of Christ is God. Every man praying or prophesying with his head covered dishonours his head and every woman who prays or prophesies with her head uncovered dishonours her head[1] – it is the same as having her hair shaved off. But if a woman does not cover her head, she should have her hair cut off, and if it is a disgrace for a woman to have her hair cut off or a shaven head, let her wear a veil.[2] A man ought not

[1] Christian custom is still for men to show respect by uncovering their heads and women by covering theirs. While modern Jewish custom is to cover one's head, this would not have been the custom in Judea in the time of Paul. The Jewish concept of head cover as a sign of humility and respect was of Babylonian origin.
[2] A woman's head of hair was, and still is, considered seductive. Rabbinic treatment, therefore, allowed young women to show off their hair until they were married. After marriage, their hair should not be displayed publicly as it could be a temptation for other men.

to cover his head since he is in the image and glory of God, but the woman is in the glory of man, for man did not come from woman, but woman came from man; nor was man created for woman, but woman was created for man. Therefore a woman, out of respect for divine authority, should have the sign of **man's** authority on her head.

In the sight of the Lord, however, there is no difference in the status between man and woman, for just as woman was created out of man, so is man born out of a woman – and the source of all is God. Judge for yourselves. Do you think it proper for a woman to pray to God with her head uncovered? Don't your natural instincts tell you that a man with long hair disgraces himself, but a woman's long hair is her glory. It is given her as **her natural** covering. **Therefore, when she prays, she should show her humility by placing a veil over her hair.** While one may quarrel over this, there is no other acceptable custom during worship for me or for the other communities of God.

In the area of the following guide lines, I **am afraid that** I am not able to command you, for your communal meetings seem to do more harm than good. First, I hear that, when you come together as a holy community, you are cliquish, and at least in part I believe it. Of course, it is natural for there to be among you different groups with **their own approaches to serving the Lord,** so that he may reveal those of whom he approves. **In your case, however, the divisions are so great that,** when you join together, it can not be said that you are eating the Lord's supper. Each one of you takes his own supper and starts eating **without regard to others.** So while one is still hungry another is already **sated and** drunk. **If you are not coming to eat as the Lord's community**, don't you have homes in which to eat and drink, or is it that you despise the community of God and enjoy embarrassing the poor among you! What do you expect me to say to you; do you expect praise? For this, I certainly cannot praise you.

"This is my body which is for you . . ."

What I have received from the Lord, I have passed on to you: The Lord Jesus on the night of his betrayal after giving thanks **to God**, broke bread and said, "This is my body which is for you.[1] Do this in remembrance of me." In the same way he took the cup after supper and said, "This cup is the new covenant sealed by my blood. Do this, as often as you drink from it, in remembrance of me. For, whenever you eat this bread and drink from this cup, you proclaim the Lord's death until he returns."

So, whoever eats the bread or drinks from the cup disrespectfully is guilty for sinning against the body and blood of the Lord. So let everyone examine himself before he lets himself eat of the bread and drink of the cup, for he who eats and drinks without recognising **it is a memorial of** the **Lord's** body, he is eating and drinking his own condemnation. That is why many among you are feeble and ill – some even having died. But, if we troubled to judge ourselves, we would not be condemned. When the Lord judges us, we are disciplined so that **on the day of judgement** we will not be condemned with the rest of the world. So, my brothers, when you come together to eat, wait for each other. If anyone is too hungry **to wait**, let him eat at home, so that when we meet together it does not lead to your condemnation. As for the other matters **you have raised,** I will settle these in person when I visit you.

Now on spiritual issues, brothers, I must not let you be ignorant. You know that when you were still Gentiles you were drawn to mute idols. Therefore I tell you that no one speaking through the divine spirit says, "Jesus be cursed" nor can one say Jesus is Lord except by means of the divine spirit.[2]

The spiritual gifts will vary

But come from the same spiritual source

---

[1] Other Greek texts have "broken for you".

[2] This is a challenging passage. I think Paul is saying that any judgement of Jesus can only be made on the basis of the gift of divine inspiration, and the validity of these judgements will depend on the extent of the gift of the divine gift (charisma) granted to the individual.

The services **of worship** will vary
But the Lord **whom they serve** is the same.
But the same God is acting through them all.

The manifestation of the spirit to one person is intended for the good of all. One, through the spirit, receives wisdom, another receives knowledge – both from the same spiritual source; to another faith from the same spirit; to another the gift of healing from the one spirit; to another the performance of wonders; to another prophecy; to another the knowledge of divine spirits; to another the gift of ecstatic utterances[1] of various kinds; and to yet another ability to interpret their meaning. All these are the work **and inspiration** of the one and same spiritual being, giving to each as he desires.

Just as the body is an integral entity but with many parts – all its many parts make up one body – so is the Christ. Indeed, through one spirit we were all baptised into one body, whether Jews or Hellenists, whether slaves or free men – we were all given to drink through one spiritual source. The body is not one member but many. If the foot were to say, "Because I am not a hand, I do not belong to the body," that statement makes him no less part of the body. And if the ear should say, "Because I am not an eye, I do not belong to the body," by saying this, it becomes no less a part of the body. If the whole body consisted of an eye, how could it hear or smell. But God has set each of the members into the body as he wished. If he only made one member where would the body be. Just so there are many different parts but only one body.

Equally, the eye cannot say to the hand, "I have no need of you," nor the head to the feet, "I have no need of you." Quite the opposite; those parts of the body which appear are even more

[1] Literally: "Speaking in tongues". I prefer the New English Bible translation which suggest individuals capable of mystical experiences revealed by ecstatic chanting. In Acts the disciples "speaking in tongues" are speaking in various languages which they had no way of knowing without divine inspiration, but which are understood by their foreign audience. Paul's reasons for preferring prophecy over speaking in tongues (see further on p. 27) indicates that we are here dealing with ecstatic mystical experiences. Having established this interpretation for the reader, I will revert to the literal "speaking in tongues" because of its literary resonance.

necessary; and those parts which are less honourable we treat with greater respect, and the unseemly part we treat with special propriety.[1] God has arranged the body by giving honour to those parts that lacked it, so that there should be no differences within the body, but that all the parts should care equally for each other. If one part suffers, every part shares its suffering. If one part is honoured, all share in its rejoicing.

Thus you are the body of Christ – each of a part of it. In the holy community – **the body of Christ** – God placed the apostles first, secondly prophets, thirdly teachers, then those with miraculous powers, then healers, then pastors, then administrators, then those who can speak in "tongues". Are all apostles, are all prophets, are all teachers, are all miracle workers, are all healers, can all speak in "many tongues", can all interpret these? Do strive for the greatest spiritual gifts, but I will show you now even the best way.

"And the greatest of these is love"

Though I speak in the languages of all men and divinities,
But speak without love, I become a clamouring gong,
Or a tinkling cymbal. If I have the gift of prophecy
And understand all the mysteries, and all knowledge –
Though I have the faith to move mountains
But I do not have love, I am nothing.
If I give away all my goods to the poor
If I offer up my body to be burnt
But have not love, I gain nothing.
Love is long-suffering
Love is giving
Love is not possessive
It does not boast nor is it arrogant.
It is not rude nor is it selfish
It does not take offence nor does it store up grievances

---

[1] An excellent metaphor to prove that the "lower ranks" in the holy community deserve even greater respect than those who are in superior positions.

Love does not gloat over the sins of others but rejoices in truth.
It bears all things; it is always trusting;
It is always hopeful; it is enduring.
Love never fails.
Prophecies cease
Languages will be forgotten
Knowledge will pass away.
In some measure we know
In some measure we prophesy
When the perfect whole arrives
The imperfect disappears.
When I was a child I spoke as a child; I thought as a child;
I reasoned as a child. When I became a man,
I put away childish things
We see through a mirror puzzling reflections
Soon we will see face to face
Now I know imperfectly
Soon my knowledge will be full
Even as I will be fully known.

But, as for now, we have three things:
Faith, hope, love –

And the greatest of these is love.

So make love your major **spiritual** goal, but still strive for other spiritual gifts, preferably the gift of prophecy[1] **over the gift of speaking in "tongues".** For the person speaking in "tongues" does not speak to men but to God because no one understands him – through divine inspiration, he speaks mysteriously; but the one who prophesies speaks to people, to teach, to encourage and to console them. He who speaks in "tongues" teaches himself, but

[1] By prophecy, Paul means the type of prophecy articulated by Isaiah and Jeremiah, etc. They were not fortune- tellers but poetic moralists who spoke out of love to those they were addressing. Any of their predictions of the course of the future would be based on their analysis of the consequences of the behaviour of their contemporaries.

he who prophesies teaches the holy community. Of course, I would like all of you to be able to speak in "tongues" **for this would give you the joy of divine inspiration**, but I would prefer that you could prophesy for he who prophesies is more beneficial **to the holy community** than he who speaks in "tongues" unless he is able to explain so that the holy community may learn **from his experience.**

For consider, brothers, were I to come to you speaking in tongues, how would you benefit, unless I bring you some revelation, knowledge, prophecy or teaching. Even when inanimate instruments render sounds – a flute or harp – unless there is a distinction in the sounds, how will anyone know what tune is being fluted or strummed? Also, if a trumpet gives an unclear call, who will prepare himself for battle? Equally, unless you who speak in "tongues" make sense, how will anyone understand what you are saying. You will just be speaking to the air. There are many different languages in the world and not one is meaningless. But, if I do not know the meaning of the words, I will be to the one speaking a foreigner, as the one speaking will be a foreigner for me. So, as you are zealous in the achievement of spiritual qualities, seek to excel in those which build up the community.

This being so, let the one who speaks in "tongues" pray for the power to explain what he is saying. When I pray in "tongues", it is my inner spirit which is praying but my mind is not working. What must I do? I will pray both with my spirit and my mind; and I will sing both with my spirit and my mind. Otherwise, if you praise God only with your spirit **by the speaking of tongues,** how can those unable to comprehend your words say "amen" to your thanksgiving if they do not know what you are saying? You do well to give thanks, but the others receive no benefit. I thank God that I speak more in "tongues" than any of you, but when I am within the holy community I would rather speak five intelligible words for the instruction of others than ten thousand words in "tongues" **which are incomprehensible**.

Brothers, stop thinking like children. In regard to evil, be as innocent as children, but in your thoughts be as grown-ups. It says in the Law[1], "In strange tongues and in a foreign language I will speak to this people and even so they will not listen, says the LORD" [Isaiah 28:11-12]. Speaking in "tongues", therefore, is a sign of God for believers but not non-believers while prophecy is of greater inspiration for non-believers than for those who **already** believe.[2] For if the entire holy community were to come together and were all to speak in tongues and an outsider or a non-believer were to enter **and hear them**, would they not conclude that you are raving mad? But if all of you were prophesying and an outsider or non-believer were to enter, and hears from everyone something which tests his conscience or takes him to account or leads him to lay bare the secrets of his soul, might he not prostrate himself and worship and affirm that God is among you! What shall we then say? Therefore, when you come together, let each one contribute a psalm or a teaching or a revelation he has had or a mystical experience or its interpretation – all ways to build up the holy community.

If there is anyone speaking in "tongues" – two, but no more than three, should speak, and **not together but** in turn; and someone must explain. If there is no one able to interpret, the speaker should keep silent in the community; let him speak to himself and God, **preferably at home.** As for prophets, let two or three speak and let the others be very attentive. But, if someone who is sitting in the audience has a sudden revelation, the speaker should stop **and make way for the one with the new revelation.** For all of you can as individuals prophesy, so that all may learn **from each other** and be encouraged **by each other.** Their prophetic spirit must be under the control of the prophet, for **they must know** that God is not a God of cacophony but of harmony.

As in all the communities of the holy, let the women in the

---

[1] It is strange that Paul identifies prophetic writings with the Torah. Perhaps the books of the Bible had not yet been differentiated, but this is unlikely.
[2] I am reversing the text: believers for non-believers and vice versa, in order to make it consistent with what Paul says in the next few verses. In this, I follow J B Phillips who only in this instance departed from the accepted text because, as he writes in his footnote: he had to conclude "that we have here either a slip of the pen on the part of Paul, or more probably, a copyist's error." [*The New Testament in Four Versions* p.535]

meeting places be silent. It is not permitted for them to speak **publicly.** They are subordinate to men, as the Torah says. If they want to learn about anything, they should ask their husbands at home. It is unseemly for a woman to speak at a holy community meeting.[1]

Did the word of God only originate with you! Are you the only people it reached? Therefore, if anyone thinks that he is a prophet or a man of the spirit, let him recognise that what I have written to you is by the LORD's command. As for the ignorant – their fate is to remain ignorant!

Therefore, brothers, be eager to prophesy, but do not forbid the speaking in "tongues". But let everything be structured in an appropriate and orderly manner.

Now, brothers, allow me to reiterate the good tidings I have preached to you which you have already received and on which basis you act. By these good tidings you are saved but only if you hold fast to the teachings I have preached. Otherwise, your beliefs were in vain. First and foremost I handed on to you what I had received – that Christ died for the sins of us all according to the Scriptures, that he was buried and raised on the third day according to the Scriptures. He was seen by Peter and then by the Twelve. Afterwards, he was seen by over five hundred brothers at the same time, of whom the majority are still living, although some have died. Afterwards he was seen by James, then by all the apostles. Last of all he appeared to me but as one whose birth **to Christ** was abnormal **in its suddenness.**

I am the least of the apostles and should not even be called an apostle because I persecuted the holy community of God. But by the grace of God I am what I am and his grace towards me was not in vain, for I have worked harder than them all – **I do not take credit for this** for it was not I but the grace of God within me. No matter whether it was I or they **the other apostles** – this is what we proclaimed and this is what you believed.

Now, if Christ is proclaimed as rising from the dead, how is it said among you that there is no resurrection of the dead? Now, if the

---

[1] Paul was not a misogynist. See Introduction.

dead are not resurrected, the Christ too has not been raised; and if he has not been raised then our proclamation has been in vain. More than that, we are then revealed as false witnesses about God because we testified that God raised Christ when he did not because in fact the dead are not raised. And, if the dead are not raised, then Christ was also not raised. And if Christ has not been raised your faith is futile and you remain imprisoned by your sins. Equally, those who have died believing in Christ are utterly lost. If only for this life we have hope in Christ we are to be more pitied than all other men.

But Christ has indeed risen from the dead, and his first fruits are those who died **in Christ**. For just as death came through a man, also through a man has come the resurrection of the dead. Just as we all die through Adam so through Christ all will be made alive; but each one in the proper order: Christ the very first and next when he comes **again** those who belong to him and in the end when he hands over the kingdom to God the father, having removed every ruler, authority and power. For he must reign until he has put all his enemies underfoot. The last enemy to be removed is death, "For God has put everything under his feet" [Psalm 8:6]. Of course, when it says that all things have been subjected to his power, it is clear that this does not include him [God] who put everything under his rule. When everything has been subjected to him [Christ] then the Son himself will be made the subject of him who put everything under him, so that God may be wholly in all things.

"Let us eat and drink for tomorrow we die"

Otherwise, what is the purpose of people being baptised vicariously for the dead[1] if they are not resurrected – why should they be

[1] It would appear that during the transition period between the first to believe in Christ and the second coming, new converts were concerned that, through no fault of their own, their deceased parents or loved ones would not be able to join them in the Kingdom of God, as they never had the opportunity to be baptised in Christ. To meet this challenge, vicarious baptism must have been introduced.

baptised on their behalf. And as for us, **the living,** why do we endanger our lives every hour of the day. Every day I face death and I swear by the pride I take in you brothers through Jesus Christ. If, as it were, I am fighting "wild beasts" here in Ephesus for mere earthly human hopes, of what benefit is it to me? If the dead are not resurrected,

"Let us eat and drink

For tomorrow we die." [Isaiah 22:13]

(Do not be misled, "Bad company corrupts good ways." Return to a sober and righteous life and sin no more. Some of you have no knowledge of God. You should be ashamed that I need say this.)

Now, some might ask, "How are the dead raised? With what kind of body will they come?" Foolish people **who ask such** questions. What you sow does not come to life unless it first dies. When you sow, you do not sow the plant that will come but a naked grain of wheat or some other cereal. But God gives it the form he desired – to each of the seeds its own form. Equally, all flesh is not the same. There is the flesh for humanity, and another flesh for animals, another for birds and another for fish. There are also heavenly bodies and earthly bodies, and the splendour of the heavenly bodies is different from that of the earthly bodies. The sun, moon and stars each have their own splendour. Indeed, each star differs in the nature of its splendour.

The same applies to the resurrection of the dead. The body that is sown is decadent, it is raised in perfection; it is sown in dishonour, it is raised in splendour; it is sown in weakness, it is raised in power; it is sown an earthly body, it is raised a spiritual body. If there exists an earthly body, there is also a spiritual body. It is written, "The first man, Adam, became a living being" [Genesis 2:7]; the final Adam became a life-giving spirit. The spiritual body does not come first – it is the earthly, only afterwards the spiritual. The first man was created from earth – therefore earthly. The final man is created from heaven. As was the earthly man – **Adam** – so are those men of earth, and as was the man created in heaven, so are the heavenly ones. As we replicated the earthly man so shall we replicate the image of the heavenly man.[1]

This I tell you, brothers, that flesh and blood cannot inherit the Kingdom of God just as decadence cannot inherit perfection. I tell you all a mystery. We shall not all die but we will all be changed – in a moment, in the glance of an eye, at the sound of the last trumpet. The trumpet will sound and the dead will be raised in perfection. So will we be changed. The decadent will clothe itself with perfection and the mortal with eternity. And, when the decadent are clothed with perfection and the mortal with eternity, then will the written word come true: Death has been swallowed up in victory.

"Where, O death, is your victory [Isaiah 23:8]
Where, O death, is your sting" [Hosea 13:14].

Now the sting of death is sin and the power over sin is the Torah.[2] But, thanks to God, he now gives us victory through our Lord Jesus Christ. So, my beloved brothers, stand firm, be immovable, fulfil yourselves by working for the Lord, always knowing that when you labour for the Lord, you labour not in vain.

Now, as for the collection for the holy **community in Jerusalem**, just as I charged the communities in Galatia, you should do the same. On the first day of every week, let each one of you set aside according to his income, so that, upon my arrival, the collection will already be in place. When I arrive, I will give you letters **of introduction** for whomever you approve to bring your gracious gift to Jerusalem. If it is appropriate that I should also go, they will go with me.[3] After I go through Macedonia I will visit you because I will be passing through Macedonia. I may even remain with you throughout the winter so that you can assist me in preparing me for my next journey wherever it will be. I do not want to see you in only a passing visit, because I hope to spend some time with you,

---

[1] This must be Jesus.

[2] Paul is quoting a rabbinic view: "When the evil inclination grabs hold of you, drag him to the house of study [of the Torah]".

[3] Paul's organisation of funds for the support of the Jerusalem community must have given him great influence and credibility with the apostles living there. He makes certain that no money is sent without him or his introductory letters.

as long as the Lord allows. I will, however, stay at Ephesus until the Pentecost, because a great door of opportunity has opened up for me inasmuch as there are many who are opposing me.

If Timothy comes, see that he has nothing to fear while he is with you, for he is doing the work of the Lord as do I. No one should reject him. Send him off with your blessings of peace so that he may come to me, for I along with the brothers here am expecting him. As to our brother Apollos, I urged him together with the brothers here to visit you. He was, however, unwilling to go but will whenever the opportunity arises. **Until my visit** be on your guard, stand firm in the faith, be manly and be strong. Do everything with love.

One other matter: I implore you, O brothers. You know the family of Stephanus which were the first converts in Achaia and who have devoted themselves to being of service to the holy ones. I urge you to accept the authority of such individuals and to everyone who works with me. I rejoiced to see Stephanus, Fortunatus and Achaicus because they provided what was missing from you. They refreshed my spirit as they **hopefully** will yours. Give proper recognition to such men. The holy communities of Asia send their greetings. Aquila and Priscilla send you warm greetings in the Lord as does the holy community that meets in her home. All the brothers here send you greetings. **Do this for me:** greet one another with a holy kiss.

With my own hand, I, Paul write this **particular** greeting.
Let anyone who does not love the Lord be cursed.
Marana tha[1] (Come, O Lord)
The grace of the Lord Jesus be with you.
My love to all of you in Jesus Christ.

[1] Aramaic.

Second Letter to the Corinthians

FROM: *Paul, an apostle of Jesus Christ through the will of God and Timothy our brother*
TO: *The holy community of God in Corinth and to all the holy ones throughout Achaia*

Grace and peace to you from God our father and the Lord Jesus Christ. Praised be God, the father of our Lord, Jesus Christ, the father of mercies and the God of all comfort, who comforts us in all our afflictions and who enables us to comfort those in trouble through the comfort of God with which we are comforted. As the sufferings of Christ suffuse our being, so through Christ our comfort overflows **to others.**

If we are afflicted, it is for your comfort and salvation and if we are comforted, it is to comfort you who endure the same sufferings as we do. Our hope in you is strong, knowing that as you share in our sufferings so you share in our comfort. We do not want you to be ignorant, brothers, of how we have been persecuted in Asia. Our burden was almost beyond our power to endure, so that we despaired even of life. We felt in ourselves that we had been sentenced to death. But this happened, **we realise**, so that we should not have trust in ourselves but in the God who has the power to raise the dead. He has delivered us from so terrible a death – he will deliver us. For on him we set our hope that he will continue to deliver us – just as you help us by your petitions on our behalf. With so many people praying for us, there will be many giving thanks on our behalf for his generous gift of deliverance to us.

We take pride in this, that our conscience is clear that, in our relationship to the outside world and to you, we have behaved honestly and with God-inspired sincerity. We have acted not in accordance with worldly wisdom but by God's grace **and inspiration.** There is nothing in our letters to you which is beyond your comprehension or understanding. Now, as you have understood us in part, I trust that in the end you will understand us completely, so that you can take pride in us as we will take pride in you in the day of our Lord Jesus.

Because of this confidence **in you** it was my original intention to visit you first so that you might have a double benefit – namely, to visit you on my way to Macedonia, to see you again on my way back from Macedonia when you could send me off **with your blessings** to Judea. When I decided to do this, do not think it was a thoughtless decision, for when I make my plans it is not done by mere human promptings – to say in the same breath both "Yes" and "No". As sure as God is faithful our message to you is not both "Yes" and "No". For the son of God, Jesus Christ, who was proclaimed to you through myself, Silvanus and Timothy was not both "Yes" and "No". In him, Jesus, it was always – Yes. For, in him, every one of God's promises is "Yes". That is why when we give glory to God, the amen we say is through him, **Jesus Christ.**

Now it is God who has established both us and you in Christ and has anointed us by marking us with his seal, giving his spirit to us as a pledge **of that which is yet to come.** I call God as my witness, on my life, that it was in order to spare you, I did not come again to Corinth. We are not dictating the nature of your faith. We work with you to increase your joy, for you are standing firmly in your faith. So I decided not to make another visit to cause you pain. For if I cause you anguish who have I left to make me glad except those I have made to suffer. That is why I wrote to you so that when I came I should not myself be made unhappy by those who should give me joy. I had put my hopes in all of you that you would share my joy. In great distress and with an anxious heart, even with many tears, I wrote to you, not to hurt you but to let you know how great is my love for you.

If anyone did cause grief, it was not so much that he distressed me, but he has to some extent, and without exaggeration, given grief to all of you. **But, now that you have responded appropriately to that man's behaviour,** his punishment, agreed by the majority, is sufficient. Now is the time to forgive and give encouragement. Otherwise he will be swallowed by an even greater grief. I therefore beg you to confirm your love for him. My reason for writing to you before was to test whether you would be obedient in all matters. **You have passed the test.** If you choose to forgive anyone, I too forgive him. Whatever I have forgiven – were there something to forgive – I have forgiven in the name of Christ and for your sake alone. If we do not, Satan will take advantage of us. For we are not ignorant of his designs. **If a man remains unforgiven, in his grief, he will become bitter and become an easy prey for Satan.**

Also, when I came to Troas to preach the good news of Christ, I found that the Lord had opened a door for me. My spirit was, however, restless because I did not find my brother Titus there. So I said goodbye to them and went on to Macedonia. But praise be to God who always leads us to triumph through Christ and through us spreads everywhere the sweet fragrance of knowing him. To God we are the fragrance of Christ to those who are being saved and to those who will perish. To the latter we are the smell of death that leads to **spiritual** death; to the former we are the fragrance of life leading to life **even more abundant**. Who is qualified for such a task! For we are not like many who chop and change[1] the word of God **for profit**, but in Christ we speak before God with sincerity as individuals sent by God.

Do we sound as though we are beginning again to commend ourselves **to you?** Or do we require, as some do, letters of recommendation to you or from you. You are our letters **of recommendation,** you who are inscribed in our hearts. Known and read by everyone you are the revealed letter of Christ, the consequence of our ministry, inscribed not with ink but with the spirit of the living God not on tablets of stone but on the tablets of human hearts. Such confidence as ours comes through Christ before God. Not that we are ourselves competent to claim commendation for what we do. Our competence comes from God who made us the

---

[1] William Tyndale's translation [1534]. I am indebted to the Tyndale Society for proving that "choppe and change", though the first, remains the best translation of the Greek "*kapaleuontes*". It is sadly forgotten that eighty per cent of the King James version is owed to William Tynsdale who was executed for his translation in 1536.

ministers of a new covenant, not of the letter but of the spirit, for the letter kills but the spirit gives life.

Now, if the ministry **of Moses** (engraved in letters on stone)[1] could not prevent death, and had such splendour that the sons of Israel were not able to look on the face of Moses because of its glorious radiance (though it would soon fade **with his death)** will not the ministry of the divine spirit be even more glorious? If the ministry that brought condemnation **to the human race through judgement under the law** was accompanied by **divine** glory how much greater will be the glory of the ministry that brings righteousness? Indeed, the glory that once was is no longer glorious in comparison with an even greater glory. And, if that which was coming to an end came with glory, how much greater is the glory which is everlasting?

Therefore, having such a hope, we are very bold **in our speech**. We are not like Moses who put a veil over his face so that the sons of Israel should not look on him though its radiance would ultimately disappear. But their minds were closed. Even until the present day when the Old Covenant **given through Moses** is read that same veil is there. It is not lifted, for only through Christ is it taken away. So until today, whenever the Torah of Moses is being read, a veil covers their hearts. But, whenever one turns to the Lord, the veil is taken away. Now the Lord is the divine spirit and where the spirit of the Lord is – there is freedom. And we all, having our faces unveiled, reflect like mirrors the glory of the Lord and are being transformed into his likeness reflecting an even brighter glory – which comes from the Lord who is the divine spirit.

Since it is by God's mercy that we are engaged in this ministry, we do not lose heart, but we have renounced doing things secretly because they are shameful. We are not devious nor do we distort the word of God. By revealing the truth as it is, we commend ourselves to every man's conscience in the sight of God. And, if the good news we proclaim seems to be obscure, it is only for those **who blindly go** on the way to destruction. The gods of the age have

---

[1] The two tablets of the Covenant – the Ten Commandments.

blinded the minds of unbelievers so that the enlightenment of the good news of the glory of Christ who is the image of God should not shine forth for them. We are not promoting ourselves but Jesus Christ as Lord and ourselves as your servants for the sake of Jesus. For the God who ordained "Let there be light" out of darkness has made his light shine in our hearts to enlighten us with the knowledge of God's glory in the face of Christ.

"We carry in our bodies the dying Jesus"

We have this treasure in vessels of clay – **in our human bodies** – to prove that this supreme power is from God and not from us . While afflicted on all sides, we do not desist **from our proclaiming Christ;** while confused **by our situation**, we do not despair; while we are persecuted, we do not feel deserted; though we are cast down, we are not destroyed for we always carry in our body the dying Jesus so that the living Jesus may be revealed in our mortal bodies. We who are alive are always in danger of death for Jesus's sake, so that his life may be revealed in our mortal flesh. While our work makes us face death, it brings you life.

We have that same spirit of faith of which was written, "As I believed, therefore I spoke" [Psalm 116:10]. It is because we believe that we speak out, knowing that the one who raised the Lord Jesus will also raise us with Jesus and then bring us into his presence with you, **when you are raised.** All this is for your benefit so that the grace that is reaching more and more people may cause songs of thanksgiving to overflow to the glory of God. Therefore, we do not grow faint. While outwardly we may be wasting away, inwardly we are renewed day by day. Our present affliction will appear exceedingly light in comparison to the extent of that eternal glory which awaits us. So we do not consider that which we can see but that which cannot be seen, for what is seen is transitory, but what is not seen is eternal.

We know that, if the earthly tent that houses us is destroyed, we have a building from God, an eternal house in heaven not made by human hands. For, in this **earthly tent**, we groan, longing to be clothed with our heavenly home, so that being clothed we shall not be found naked. Indeed, while we are in this **mortal** tent we groan because we are burdened **by the fear of death.** We do not wish to put off **our present mortal clothing** but rather to put on **our eternal clothing,** so that our mortality may be swallowed up by **eternal** life. Now the One who has achieved this very purpose **for us** has given us his divine spirit as a surety of that **life eternal** which is to come.

We are, therefore, always in good cheer knowing that while we are at home in the mortal body we are "away from home" from the Lord. We live by faith and not by what we see. We are in good cheer because we think it better to leave the home of the body to go home to the Lord. So our ambition is to please him whether at home **in the body** or not at home. For the destiny of us all is to appear before the tribunal of Christ, so that each may receive his due according to the things he did while in his body – whether good or bad.

As we fear the Lord, we seek to persuade men **of the truth.** What we are **doing** is plain to God and hopefully plain to your con- sciences as well. **In telling you all this** we are not seeking to commend ourselves to you, but an opportunity for you to take pride in us so that you may be able to respond to those who take pride in appearances and not in the goodness of their hearts. If we appear mad, it is for the sake of God, but if we are rational, it is for you. The love of Christ demands this of us, because it is our judge- ment that one man died on behalf of us all – therefore all died **with him**. And he died for all of us so that the living no longer live for themselves but for the sake of the one who died for them and was raised again.

From now on, we consider no one on the basis of his existence as a man of flesh, and if we once regarded Christ in this way, we no longer do so. Therefore if anyone is in Christ, he is a new creation. The old has passed away – they have become new! All this comes from God who reconciled us to himself through Christ and has entrusted to us the ministry of reconciliation – God was reconcil- ing the world to himself through Christ, without holding men's sins against them. To us he has committed the message of reconciliation. Therefore, we are the ambassadors of Christ as if God were making his appeal **to the world** through us. We beg you on behalf of Christ. Be reconciled to God. The one who did not know sin, God made into a sin offering so that we might **through him** become righteous in God's **sight**.

As we are working together we plead with you not to receive the grace of God in vain, **for you may not be given another opportunity,** for he says,

"In an acceptable time I heard you
And in the day of salvation, I helped you" [Isaiah 48:9].

Now is an acceptable time. Now is the day of salvation. We put no stumbling block before anyone so that our ministry should not be at fault. Everything we did commended us as the servants of God, enduring so much – afflictions, hardships, dire straits, floggings, imprisonment, being mobbed, indefatigable work, sleeplessness and hunger; yet with innocence, knowledge, patience, kindness, holiness of spirit, sincere love, words of truth, the strength of God through an armoury of righteousness both on our right and left sides; **ministering** both in glory and dishonour, praise and blame, regarded both as deceivers and reliable men, both as non-entities and famous – on the verge of death but still alive, beaten but not killed, pained yet rejoicing, poor but enriching many others **through the spirit**, having nothing yet possessing all things.

We have opened ourselves to you, O Corinthians, we have revealed our hearts to you. We are not holding anything back from you, but you are holding back from us. As a reciprocal gesture – I say this to you as my children – open yourself **up to us.** Do not mix with unbelievers, for what can righteousness and lawlessness share, or how can light be a companion with darkness? Can Christ have an agreement with Belial, a believer with a non-believer? Can God and idols share the same shrine? For we are the shrine of the living God, as God has said,

"I will live among them and walk with them
I will be their God and they will be my people.

Therefore come away from them and be separate,"
Says the LORD, Do not touch an unclean thing
And I will welcome you.
I will be a father to you
You will be my sons and daughters," says the LORD the Almighty.[1]

As we have these promises **of salvation**, my loved ones, let us cleanse ourselves from all pollution of the flesh and of the spirit, seeking the perfection of holiness through the fear of God. Make room for us **in your hearts.** We have wronged no one. We have injured no one. We have defrauded no one. I do not say this to condemn you. I have said before that you are so much in our hearts that we would live or die with you. You have my full confidence. I take much pride in you. I am greatly comforted. In spite of all our troubles, I overflow with joy.

When we reached Macedonia, our bodies were given no rest. We had nothing but troubles: struggles without and anxiety within. But God who gives comfort to the humble comforted us – by bringing Titus; and not only by his arrival but by **the knowledge of** the comfort you had given him. He reported to us how much you missed me, your sadness **over how you had upset me** and your deep concern for me – which made me rejoice even more. If my letter caused you grief, I did not regret sending it. If the letter hurt you, I see that it was only for a short time. And now I am happy not that you felt hurt but that the hurt moved you to repentance. You suffered because of God not because of us. The sorrow that comes from God leads to repentance which leads to salvation and is not to be regretted. But worldly sorrows lead to **spiritual** death. Look at how your sorrow due to God produced in you such earnestness along with your anxiety, fear and anger and zeal to defend yourselves and that justice be done. At every point you proved yourselves innocent in this matter.

When I wrote to you **concerning this problem** it was not on account of the offender nor on behalf of the victim but in order to prove how loyal you were to us before God. We are therefore most

[1] A pot pouri of verses from the prophets.

comforted. But our sense of comfort increased even more as the consequence of our joy over Titus's delight because you all put his mind to rest. I boasted to him about you and you have not embarrassed me. So just as everything we said to you was true, so too was the pride in you which I expressed to Titus justified. And his affection for you has increased for he remembers how obedient you were and with what "fear and trembling" you welcomed him. I rejoice that I can have complete confidence in you.[1]

Now, we would like you to know, brothers, the grace of God which has been granted to the communities of Macedonia. Though severely tested by hardships, they were joyous and in spite of their extreme poverty were immensely generous. I am witness to the fact that both within and beyond their means they gave voluntarily and of their own accord imploring us for the privilege of sharing in the service of the holy ones **in Jerusalem**. Beyond our expectations, first they dedicated themselves to the Lord and then gave to us **because they perceived it** as the will of God. So, **with this example**, we urged Titus, as he had begun his work, to bring it to completion – the gift of generosity from you. Just as you excel in faith, in eloquent testimony **to Christ**, in knowledge, in sincerity and your love for us – see also that you excel in this grace **of giving.**

This is not by way of command, but through the example of the sincerity of others, to test the quality of your own love. You know of the grace of generosity of our Lord Jesus Christ, that though he was rich for your sake he impoverished himself, so that through his poverty you might become rich. This is the most practical advice I can offer you. Last year you were not only the first to give but also the first with the will to give. So carry on with the work so that your willing eagerness is matched by action and according to your means. For if the willingness to give is there, the gift is valued in relationship to what one has and not in relationship to what he does not have. The intention is not to bring relief to others while you remain in distress but to create a fair balance. At present, your

---

[1] In what follows Paul proves himself to be an extraordinary fund-raiser. His canvassing techniques cannot be surpassed.

surplus will supply what they need so that in time **if necessary** their surplus will provide you with what you may need, so that there may be equality, as it has been written: "He that gathered much did not have more that gathered a little and did not have less." [Exodus 16:18][1]

Thanks be to God who put the same concern I have for you in the mind of Titus. Not only did he accept our need for an appeal but he of his own accord went to you. We sent with him the brother who is praised by all the holy communities for his manner of proclaiming the good news. He was also elected by the holy communities to be our companion when we bear this gift which we do to honour the Lord himself and to show our desire to help. We want to avoid any blame for the way we dispense of this chari-table fund. We must be seen to act properly not only in the eyes of the Lord but also in the eyes of man.

We have also sent with them our brother who has so often proved to us in so many ways his diligence, now even more so because of his confidence in you. As for Titus, my partner and fellow worker among you, and as for our brothers **who are coming to you**, they are delegates from the holy communities which give honour to Christ. Therefore, show these men evidence of your love and the reason for our pride in you among the holy communities.

There should be no necessity for me to write to you about serving the needs of the holy ones **in Jerusalem**, as I know of your willingness and I have cited you as an example for the Macedonians, telling them that, since last year, you in Achaia were preparing for the collection and that your enthusiasm has inspired a great number of donors. I sent the brothers to make sure that my pride in you was not mistaken in regard to this, so that you were prepared as I assured them you would be; for, if any Macedonians come with me and you find you are not ready with your collection, we, and not to mention you, would be embarrassed because of the confidence we expressed. It is for this reason that I asked the brothers to visit you

[1] This is in reference to the in-gathering of the manna in the wilderness.

in advance **of my own** to redeem your pledges offered as a privilege
and not as extortion.

God loves a cheerful giver

Also remember this: the one who sows sparingly will reap little
and the one who sows generously will reap great blessings. Let
each one contribute what he has chosen in his heart to give, not
with pain and not under compulsion, because God loves a cheerful
giver. And God is able to bestow upon you great blessings, so that
at all time, having what you need, you will have enough to give to
every worthy cause, as it is written, "He disperses his gifts to the
poor, his righteousness endures in every age." [Psalm 112:9]

He who provided seed for the sower and bread for food will
enlarge your storehouse with seed and will increase the harvest of
your righteousness. You will be enriched in everything so that you
may be generous and through us your generosity will lead to
thanksgiving to God. Because the service of giving is not only pro-
viding for the needs of the holy ones but also leads to the great
songs of thanksgiving to God. Because of what you do to prove
yourselves, men will glorify God because of your submission which
you show to the good news of Christ and through your generosity
in fellowship with them and all men. Even more, when men pray
for you, they will feel drawn towards you because of the great
blessings God has given you. Thanks be to God for his blessings
which are beyond telling.

With the humility and patience of Christ, I, Paul, who am reti-
cent when facing you but aggressive when at a distance from you,
I appeal to you: I plead with you that when I am in your presence I
need not be as aggressive as I would be towards people who think
that we ought to live according to worldly standards. Though
human, we do not do battle as humans, for our weapons are not
human weapons, but they have the divine power to overthrow
strongholds. All arguments and every great obstacle which has
been raised against the knowledge of God. We employ every mode
of argument to instil obedience to Christ. We are ready to punish

any disobedience once you have affirmed full obedience **to Christ.**

Look at the facts. If anyone believes that he belongs to Christ, let him understand that just as he belongs to Christ so do we. I am not embarrassed to take pride freely in the fact that the Lord gave us the authority to bolster you and not to tear you down. It is not my intention to frighten you by my letters. They say, "His letters are weighty and strong but in person he is weak and his speeches beneath contempt." Let them appreciate that as we are in our letters when absent, so will our actions be when we are present.

We do not dare to classify ourselves among those who produce their own testimonials. They are foolish because they measure themselves by their own standards and compare themselves to each other **within their own group. How can they be objective?** We do not boast **of any authority over you** beyond that which God has set for us in regard to coming to you **with the good news.** We are not overreaching ourselves because we came such a long way to you with the good news of Christ. Nor do we take the credit for work done by others. We only hope that as your faith grows in strength our opportunity of expanding the faith will also grow, so that we can proclaim the good news in territories further afield rather than credit ourselves for the work done in someone else's territory. But, "If anyone would boast let him boast in the LORD" [Jeremiah 9:23]. For approval does not come to a man from self-commendation but comes to him from the Lord.

I would that you indulged me with a small bit of foolishness – but of course you do indulge me. If I am jealous for you, it is a jealousy on God's behalf. I betrothed you to one husband – to present you as an innocent virgin to Christ. But I fear that, just as the serpent through his cleverness deceived Eve, somehow you have been led astray from your simple and innocent thoughts about Christ. If another person comes and preaches a Jesus whom we did not proclaim or you receive a different spiritual message of the good news from the one you received from me, you tolerate it. I do not think that I am inferior to these "super-apostles". If I am not as eloquent as they, I do have more knowledge. We have made this perfectly clear to you in every way.

Was it wrong for me to demean myself by preaching the good news to you for no payment so that you might be elevated? I, so to speak, was stealing from other holy communities by taking wages so as to be in the position to serve you. When I was with you, I was not a financial burden to anyone for my needs for my brothers who came from Macedonia supported me. So I have kept myself independent of your support and so will I continue to do. So long as the truth of Christ is in me, no one in the territory of Achaia will stop me taking pride in what I am doing. Why? Is it because I do not love you! God knows that I do. I will continue to do what I am doing to cut off the ground from under the feet of those who are looking for every opportunity to prove that they are equal to us in the right to boast of being **the true apostles of Christ.**

These are false apostles, fraudulent labourers masquerading as apostles of Christ. This is not to be wondered at for does not Satan masquerade as a divine messenger of light? It is therefore not such an incredible thing if his ministers masquerade as ministers of righteousness – but their end will be as evil as their works. I say again. Let no one think me a fool. And, even if you consider me a fool, accept me as such and indulge a little bit of my conceit. When I smugly boast, I do not as would the Lord, but as a fool. Since most boast according to the standards of the world, so too will I boast. Because you believe yourselves to be so wise, you suffer fools gladly. In fact you tolerate anyone who enslaves or exploits you or takes advantage of you, or who sets himself above you or even slaps you in the face. To my shame I must confess that we were too weak to assert this **power over you.**

"When anyone is weak, do I not feel weak?"

Whatever anyone else has the effrontery to boast about – I know I am now speaking like a fool – I too can boast of. Are they Hebrews?[1] I am too! Are they Israelites? I am too! Are they of the

---

[1] Paul must be referring to the Jews believing in Christ who, unlike himself, insisted that conversion to Christ was not possible without circumcision.

descendants of Abraham? I am too! Are they servants of Christ? (I am out of my mind to go on like this.) I am a greater servant than are they. I have worked with greater intensity, been in prison more frequently, flogged more excessively and threatened by death many times. From the Jews I received five times the "forty lashes minus one". Three times have I been smitten by rods. Once was I stoned. Three times was I shipwrecked – I spent a whole day and night floundering in the open sea. I have been constantly on the move. I have been in danger from rivers, in danger from robbers, in danger from my own countrymen, in danger from Gentiles, in danger in towns, in danger in the country, in danger in the sea, in danger from deceiving brothers. I have worked and toiled, sleeplessly waiting for morning many times, in famine and thirst often going without food and being cold and naked. And apart from all this I have the worries every day of caring for all the holy communities. When anyone is weak, do I not feel weak! When anyone is led into sin, do not I burn **internally as if I had been the sinner!**

If I boast, it is to boast of my weaknesses. The God and father of the Lord Jesus, he who is forever praised, knows that I am not lying. In Damascus, the ethnarch under King Aretas kept watch over the city of the Damascenes to arrest me. It was only by being lowered in a basket through a window in a wall that I slipped through his hands.

I will go on boasting **of what I have done,** even if there is nothing to be gained: I will speak now of the visions and revelations from the Lord **which have been granted to me.** I have heard of a man in Christ who fourteen years ago – whether in the body or separated from his body, I do not know, only God knows – was lifted up into the third heaven. I have heard that this man – whether in the body or separated from his body, I do not know, only God knows – was lifted up into Paradise. He heard words which cannot be described and which a person would not be permitted to speak. Of such a man's experience I will boast, but not of my own, except it be on my frailties.

Even if I chose to boast **of visions and revelations,** I would not be acting the fool, for I would be telling the truth, but I refrain from doing this because I only want people to think of me on the basis of what he has seen me do or have heard from others and not on the basis of the many revelations **which have been granted to me and of which I could report to you**. To prevent me from being exalted **by this gift**, Satan sent a messenger to become a thorn in my flesh[1], to batter me so that I would not rise above myself. Three times I implored the Lord to release me from it. But he said to me, "Be satisfied that you live in my grace, for my power through weakness is perfected; **through your torment will my power in you be made stronger**." Therefore, I even gladly boast of my weaknesses for because of them the power of Christ dwells in me. Therefore I take pleasure in weaknesses, in insults, in hardships, in persecutions and in difficulties – all for the sake of Christ, for when I am weak I am strong.

If I have made a fool of myself, you drove me to it. You ought to have commended me **so that I would not have needed to commend myself**, for I lack nothing of what the super-apostles[2] have, even though I am nothing. The signs that prove an apostle were done among you with utmost devotion and patience, namely, by signs, wonders and mighty deeds. For in what way were you treated **by me** with less consideration than the other holy communities, except that I never was a burden upon your resources. Forgive me for wronging you in this way.[3]

Now I am ready to visit you for a third time and I will not be a burden to you because it is you and not what you have that I seek. Children do not save up for their parents but parents save for their children. So I am most glad to spend and be spent out for the sake of your souls. If I love you more will you love me less? Let it pass. I

[1] He is referring to unspecified physical ailments of an unrelenting nature.

[2] The reader may wince at this word but it is the literal translation of the Greek *uperlian*. I think it an appropriate translation because Paul, feeling that he is as great an apostle as the others denigrates them by going "over the top" in referring to them. I am not alone in translating it this way. Others: chief, superlative, extra special.

[3] Paul's irony is delicious. He seems to appreciate the fact that they resent his independence.

have been a burden to you. **Would you say then** that I seduced you through craftiness and trickery? I did not take advantage of you through anyone I sent to you. I urged Titus to visit you and sent a brother with him. Did Titus cheat you? Did he not behave towards you with the same spirit as myself and did he not walk in my steps?

You think that we are defending ourselves to you, but it is before God that we speak, my beloved ones; all we do is on your behalf in order to strengthen you. I am anxious that when I arrive I will not find you as I want you to be and you may not find me as you would like. I anticipate quarrels, resentment, anger, conflict, malicious gossip, pride and disorder. I am afraid that, when I come again, my God will humble me before you **because of your behaviour** and I will be upset over those who have sinned earlier and who have not repented over their impurity, licentiousness and debauchery, which they have committed.

This will be the third time I will be coming to you. "By the mouth of two or three witnesses every charge is established" [Deuteronomy 19:15]. Previously, on my second visit, I gave you a personal warning. Now being away, I reiterate it. When I return I will not spare those who have sinned before or the others who have sinned since. Since you are looking for proof that Christ speaks through me, **you will see** he will not be weak towards you but harsh. Indeed he was crucified in weakness, yet now he lives by God's power. And indeed while we are weak **in his weakness**, we shall live with him also in the power which he will **through me** reveal to you.

Examine yourselves. Are you living in the faith? Put yourself to the test. Do you yourself feel that Jesus Christ is in you or are you counterfeit? You, I trust, will know that we are not counterfeit. Now we pray to God that you do nothing wrong. It is not for us to win approval **from God** but only that you do what is right, even though we may appear as failures **in the influence we have had on you.** We have no power to resist the truth – only to further it. We are satisfied with our weakness so long as you are strong, and our prayer is for your perfect spiritual fulfilment. This is why I write this to you when I am away so that, when I am with you in person,

I need not treat you harshly according to the authority granted me by the LORD – rather to build you up than to destroy you.

Finally, brothers, rejoice! Mend your ways! Encourage each other! Be one in mind and spirit! Live in peace! The God of love and peace be with you. Greet one another with a holy kiss. All the holy ones send you their greetings. May the grace of the Lord Jesus Christ and the love of God and the fellowship which is ours in the divine spirit be with all of you.

Letter to the Galatians

FROM: *Paul, an apostle – not sent by men nor by a man but by Jesus Christ and God the father, who is he who raised him from the dead – and with me all the brothers, to the holy communities of Galatia.*
TO: *The holy communities of Galatia:*
Grace and peace to you from God our father and Lord Jesus Christ, he who gave himself because of our sins so that he may deliver us out of the present evil age according to the will of our God and father, to whom be glory for ever and ever. Amen.

I am amazed that so quickly you have forsaken the one who **first** called you by the grace of Christ and are turning to a different teaching of the good news, not that there can be any other! There are trouble-makers among you who are seeking to pervert the good news of Christ. Even we or a messenger out of heaven who proclaims good news other than that which we have preached to you – let him be accursed! As we have said before and as I say again: if anyone preaches a version of the good news other than what you have already received – let him be accursed! Whom am I trying to convince now, men or God? Am I trying to please human beings? If I wanted to please men, I would not have become a servant of Christ.

For I make known to you, brothers, the good news I preach is not from man. I did not receive it from man but through the revelation of Jesus Christ. You have heard of how I practised my Judaism, how I went to extremes in persecuting the community of God and tried to destroy it; and how I went further than the Jews of my generation in my fanatical zeal for the tradition of my ancestors. But when God chose me, from the moment I came out of my mother's womb and called me through his grace to reveal his son in me so that I might preach him among the Gentiles, I did not consult anyone, nor did I go up to Jerusalem to see those who were apostles before me, but I went into Arabia and returned again to Damascus. After three years I went up to Jerusalem to see Peter and stayed with him for fifteen days. I did not meet the other apostles except for James, the Lord's brother.

Now what I am writing to you is before God, so I do not lie. Then I went into the regions of Syria and Cilicia. I was personally unknown to the holy communities of Judea who are in Christ. They only heard: "The one who had formerly been persecuting us is now preaching the faith he sought to destroy," and they glorified God because of me **and my conversion**.

Fourteen years later I went up again to Jerusalem with Barnabas and with Titus. I went up because of a revelation and I put before them the good news which I was preaching to the Gentiles – privately and only to recognised leaders, to make certain that **what I was doing and had done** – all my rushing around then and now – was not for nothing. Nor was my companion Titus – though a Hellenist – required to be circumcised. **The matter arose** because false brothers secretly infiltrated in order to spy on the freedom we gained through Christ in order to enslave **us through rites and practices, especially circumcision.** We did not yield one inch in compromise so that the truth of the good news could be realised in you.[1]

Those who seemed to have some authority[2] – of what kind of status they enjoyed is of no consequence to me for God is not concerned about human position – added nothing to my teaching. Quite the opposite, they saw that I had been entrusted with the task of bringing the good news to the uncircumcised as Peter was entrusted with the apostleship to the circumcised. As the one who was working through Peter for the circumcised was also working through me for the Gentiles. James, Peter and John, the seeming pillars **of the community**, acknowledging the grace given to me, extended to me and Barnabas their right hands in fellowship so that we should go to the Gentiles, as they would to the circumcised

[1] Paul appears to be saying that the Jewish believers were requiring circumcision of pagan believers before accepting them into the community of Christ. Paul explains that such a demand would limit the numbers of converts to Christ.

[2] Paul here and previously seems to dismiss the importance of the leadership in Jerusalem. The Greek text refers to the leaders he addresses as "the ones seeming [to be leaders]." Translators have added "reputed individuals" or "acknowledged leaders" etc. Is he maintaining that only he has the true message?

– but that we should also remember the poor in Jerusalem, something I was eager to do **in any event.**

"I opposed Peter face to face"

When Peter came to Antioch I opposed him face to face because he was wrong **according to his own previous judgement.**[1] Before certain people sent by James came **to protest to** Peter about his **non-observance of Jewish practices,** he used to eat **unclean meat** with the Gentiles[2], but after they came he drew back and separated himself from the Gentiles being afraid of those who insisted on circumcision. The other Jews also joined him in his hypocrisy **because they continued to eat unclean foods.** Even Barnabas was led astray by their hypocrisy.[3] When I saw that they were not walking in line with the truth of the good news, I protested to Peter in front of them all, saying, "You are a Jew, living as a Gentile and not as a Jew. How is it then that you force Gentiles to follow Jewish customs **if they wish to become believers?"**

We who are Jews by birth and not Gentile sinners still know that a man is not acquitted of guilt by observing the Torah, but through faith in Jesus Christ. So we too believe in Jesus Christ so that we may be acquitted by faith in Christ and not through the observance of the Torah. Because **as we know** by the observance of the Torah, no mortals can achieve acquittal, for **"who can say, "I am**

[1] This is a very significant passage as it indicates the deep division between the Jerusalem believers who remained a Jewish sect led by Peter and the Gentiles led by Paul. There is no record of this meeting in Acts. There we only have evidence of the full agreement between Paul and Peter that neither circumcision nor the mass of Jewish ritual practice should be required of those Gentiles who believed in Christ [Chapter 15]. Paul, however, in spite of this continued to maintain that he remained Jewish and indeed boasts of it in other letters.

[2] See Acts Chapters 10 and 11. It is significant that it is James, Jesus's brother, who wants to maintain full Jewish observance.

[3] Acts reports a deep disagreement between Paul and Barnabas which leads to their separation. Ostensibly, it is because the latter wanted John to accompany them on their mission. [Acts 15:36-40]. This seems to be the real reason. The author of Acts in his desire to reconcile the different wings of the new faith glosses over this deep difference in approach.

pure **from sin?'"** [[Proverbs 20:9]. But suppose you were to say that, by believing in our acquittal **of guilt** through Christ, we then took license to become sinners **by immoral practice,** then Christ is the source of our sinfulness – let it not be so!

Now, were I to restore the building – that is the belief that by obedience to the Torah we acquit ourselves from sin – I prove that I am a transgressor but of a higher law, that is to achieve righteousness through faith in Christ. It was through the Torah – the knowledge that I could not find salvation in the Torah – that I died to the Torah, that I rejected it as the source of my salvation, so that I might live in God through the acceptance of his spirit through Christ. With Christ, I have been jointly crucified and no longer live as myself but Christ lives in me. The life I live in my body, I live only by faith in the Son-of-God, who in his love for me gave himself up to death for me. I cannot discount the grace of God in what Christ did for us for if, through obedience of the Torah, righteousness and the acquittal from sin is achieved, then Christ died for nothing.[1]

O foolish Galatians. Jesus Christ is reported as crucified by everyone – even by those who have now bewitched you. Tell me one thing: was it instruction in the Torah or was it by belief in the message **of Christ** that you received the spirit? So are you not foolish then? Having begun with the spirit**ual message of salvation through the death and resurrection of Christ,** are you now reverting to seek to perfect yourself through human effort – **by observing the Torah?** Have you suffered so much in vain – if indeed it was in vain? Does God who gives you his spirit and works wonders before you do this because you observe the Torah or because of your faith in what you heard?

As Abraham's belief in God was called righteousness, know then that those who believe, **and not those who only obey the Torah,** are the sons of Abraham. The writings foresaw that God would acquit the Gentiles through faith, for he announced the good news first to Abraham: "all nations will be blessed in you"

---

[1] This is the heart of the matter. The mystery of Christ replaces the Torah as the basis of human salvation both in this world and in the next.

[Genesis 12:3; 18:18; 22:18]. So are those of faith blessed together with the believer Abraham. All who trust in the observance of the Torah are under a curse, for it has been written, "Cursed is everyone who does not continue to do all that has been written in the scroll of the Torah" [Deuteronomy 27:26].

It is clear that no man is acquitted before God by keeping the Torah because, "the righteous live by faith." And the Torah is not based on faith, because it is written, "The one who observes them [the laws] will live by them, **and not by faith.**" Christ redeemed us from the curse of the Torah – **in that no one who is under the Torah can help but be cursed because he cannot be acquitted from sin through observing it** – by becoming himself a curse for our sake, as it has been written, "Accursed is everyone who hangs on a tree" [Deuteronomy 21:23].[1] **God did this** so that the blessing given to Abraham might come to the Gentiles through Jesus Christ so that by faith we would receive the divine spirit.

Brothers, let me cite an everyday example **to prove my point.** Once a contract has been made, no one can add or subtract from it. Just so when God said to Abraham he would grant his promises to his descendant it does not say "to his descendants" which would suggest many. So here he is referring to only one; who is Abraham's one seed? It is Christ. Now my meaning is this: the Torah introduced four hundred and thirty years later **at Sinai** does not annul the covenant with Abraham which had been previously ratified by God – the promise **regarding Abraham's descendant** is not superseded. You see, if the inheritance **of Abraham's blessing** comes through the Torah, it does not come through the promise

---

[1] This is shocking proof text. The law is against hanging anyone on a tree for more than a day without burial. It is intended as a warning against the executioner, not the executed. The ambiguity of the wording allows Paul to say that the crucified Christ not only died for human sin but took on himself the human curse through his "rejection" of the Torah, by the fact that he "hung on a tree". Of course, Jesus did not hang on a tree but was nailed to a cross. Significantly, it is only in Acts that Jesus is reported three times to have been hung on a tree. Its author, Luke, a follower of Paul, must have employed this phraseology in order to validate Paul's argument here. In the light of this new speculation, I must ask my readers to ignore my footnote No. 2 on p. 112 on the same subject in *St Luke and The Apostles.*

**based on Abraham's faith and not on the Torah as Abraham did
not live under the Torah.** But God gave his blessing to him through
a promise.

What then, **you may ask**, was the purpose of the Torah. It was
given to deal with transgressions until the descendant to whom
the promise was made had come. The Torah was ordained by
Messengers from God through the hand of a mediator **(Moses).
Now a mediator is required by two parties, to make a contract or
covenant between them, and the Torah is the scroll of the
covenant. So Moses was the mediator between God's Messengers
and the Israelites.** But a mediator is not required where there is
only one party, and God being one **did not need a mediator when
he made his promise to Abraham.**

Is the Torah, then, in contradiction to the promises of God? Not
at all. If the Torah that was given could impart **eternal** life, then
saving righteousness would have come through the Torah. But
the writings say that the whole world is subject to sin, so that the
promise of **saving** faith in Jesus Christ was given to those who
believe. Before faith came, we were in custody and subject to the
Torah until faith was revealed. So the Torah was our trainer until
Christ came when we could be acquitted of sin through faith.
And now that faith has come we no longer require the Torah as
our trainer.

"There is neither Jew nor Hellenist"

You are all sons of God through faith in Jesus Christ, for all of you
who were baptised in Christ are clothed in Christ. There is neither
Jew nor Hellenist; there is neither slave nor freeman; there is
neither male nor female – for you are all one in Jesus Christ. And if
you are of Christ then you are Abraham's descendants and heirs
according to his promise. I say this, but so long as an heir is an
infant, he differs in no way from a slave even though he be the lord
of the manor. He is subject to guardians and trustees until the time
set by his father **for him to come into his inheritance.** So in our case:
when we were infants we were subject to the basic elements of

nature. When in the fullness of time God sent forth his son, born of woman subject to the Torah, he did so in order to ransom those subject to the Torah so that we would receive the rights of adopted sons. And, because you are sons, God sent the divine spirit of his son into our hearts who calls out *Abba* – father! So you are no longer a slave but a son; and if a son, then also an heir of God, **our father.**

But when you did not know God you were "enslaved" to beings who were no-gods but now knowing God – even better, being known by God, why would you turn again to those weak and miserable principles? Do you wish to serve them once again? You are **religiously** observing special days, months, seasons and years. I fear for you that in vain have I worked for you. **As we belong to Christ every day belongs to Christ – and every day is special.**

I plead with you, brothers: put yourself into my place as I put myself into yours. You have not wronged me in any way. You know that it was because of a physical illness, I first preached the good news to you. While my condition put you to the test, **on seeing the state of my body** you neither despised nor scorned me. You welcomed me as a Messenger from God, even as Jesus Christ. What has become of the joy you felt then? I can testify that, if you could have done so, you would have torn out your eyes for me. Is it that I have become your enemy because I speak the truth to you?

Those people are devoted to you but not for your own good. What they wish is to separate you from me so that you will be devoted to them. It is a good thing always to be devoted to that which is good and not only when I am with you. My children, for whom I again feel the pains of childbirth until Christ is **once** again in you, how I wish I could be with you now and to change my tone towards you. But I am confused by you.[1]

[1] The vehemence of Paul's attack suggests that those calling on believers to be circumcised and to observe the Torah were having some success among the Gentiles. This is impressive as Jewish observances would have been very demanding on them. Is it that they felt some need for collective practices, some material rituals in addition to faith. Remember that, in these early days, the rituals would have been very simple and basic, especially if the Torah was being ignored. There would have been no Christmas, Easter, Lent, etc.

Tell me, those of you who wish to be under the Torah, have you not heard what the Torah says? It has been written that Abraham had two sons, one from a maidservant and one from a free woman. The one from the maidservant had been born naturally; the one from the free woman through a **divine** promise, **for Sarah being ninety years old was beyond the age of child bearing.** These events can be interpreted as an allegory, for these represent two covenants, one from Mount Sinai which gives birth to slaves – that is **the descendants of** Hagar, **the maidservant.** Now Hagar symbolises Mount Sinai which is in Arabia and corresponds to the physical Jerusalem. She is in slavery with her children, **for they are subject both to the Romans and the Torah.** But the Jerusalem above – **the heavenly Jerusalem** – is free, and she is our mother, as it is written,

"Sing O barren woman who has not borne.
Break out into song and shout you who have not gone into labour,
For more numerous are the children of the deserted **woman**
Than of her who has a husband." [Isaiah 54:1]

Now, you brothers, like Isaac, are the children of promise. But even as then the son naturally born persecuted the one born by **the promise of** the divine spirit, so now too. But what do the Writings say? "Cast out the maidservant and her son for the son of the maidservant will by no means inherit with the son of the free woman" [Genesis 21:10]. Therefore, brothers, we are not of the children of the maidservant but of the free woman.[1]

To give us freedom has Christ set us free. Therefore, stand firm and do not be entangled again with the yoke of slavery **which is the Torah.** See, I Paul tell you that, if you be circumcised, Christ will be of no benefit to you. Furthermore, and I confirm again, every man who is circumcised becomes obliged to obey the entire Torah. You who seek to be acquitted **from sin by** observing the

---

[1] An ironic twist by Paul: the Jews who are descendants of Isaac, because they are subject to the Torah are identified with Ishmael, the son of Hagar, the slave woman whose descendants were not in fact subject to the Torah, while the believing Gentiles who did not observe the Torah are identified with Isaac who was the ancestor of those who were subject to the Torah.

Torah cut yourselves off from Christ and fall away from his grace. Led by the divine spirit, we through faith hope to achieve the saving justice for which we are waiting with such anticipation. For in Jesus Christ neither circumcision nor non-circumcision has any relevance – only faith which works through **God's** love.

You were doing so well; you were running a good race. Who put an obstacle in your way to stop you from reaching the truth. Whatever persuasion was used did not come from God who had called you. A little yeast ferments the whole batch of dough.[1] **Thus a minimum of false information can ruin all that you have achieved.** I trust in the Lord that you will agree with me; and that the one who has worried you – **saying that you need be circumcised** – shall be punished whoever he may be. If I, brothers, am still advocating circumcision[2] **as some people allege**, why am I being persecuted? **If I were to insist that in order to receive the grace of Christ, one had to become one of the Jews through circumcision,** would the cross cease to cause offence, **by which we teach that the Lord Jesus Christ died so that we could die to sin and was raised so that we could be raised to life now and in the day of judgement.** As for those trouble makers **who urge you to be circumcised**, let them go and castrate themselves!

You, brothers, were called to freedom, but not for the permissiveness of the flesh, but through this freedom to serve each other in love. For the whole Torah was summed up in one command: "You shall love your neighbour as yourself" [Leviticus 19:18]. But if you bite and consume each other, beware, for you will destroy each other. I say walk with the spirit and you will not obey the lustful passions of the flesh **which is the cause of sin and for which the Torah was given.** The desires of the flesh are in battle with the spirit and the spirit does battle against the desires of the flesh. One

---

[1] Yeast was symbolically identified with evil. Before Passover, Jews removed all yeast from their homes, and only unleavened bread – *Matzah* – may be eaten. The wafer of the Eucharist is a symbol of the *matzah*, which in turn is identified with the flesh of Jesus.

[2] He did have Timothy circumcised in order to please the Jews; see Acts 16:1-3. Remember what Paul says: To the Jews I am a Jew, see p. 19

opposes the other. Otherwise you would do whatever you desired. So long as you are guided by the divine spirit there is no need for you to be subject to the Torah.

The sinful acts of the flesh are obvious **to anyone. We do not need the Torah to know what they are** – sexual licentiousness, impurity, perversity, idolatry, sorcery, hostility, strife, envy, anger, quarrels, dissension, factions, malicious envy, drunkenness, orgies and the like. I have already warned you, as I did before, that those who indulge in such practices will not inherit the Kingdom of God. But the fruit of the spirit is love, joy, peace, patience, kindness, goodness, faithfulness, humility, self-control. The Torah is not against these virtues, **but does not have the power to order them to become part of us.** Those who belong to Christ have crucified the flesh with its passion and lustfulness, **and have no need for the Torah.** If we live in the spirit, let us also walk with the spirit. Let us not be arrogant, provoking and envying each other.

Brothers, if a person is caught up in a sinful action, you who are with the spirit should restore such a person ever so gently **to moral** behaviour. But be careful, **do not be smug in your own righteousness,** for you could be tempted **to sin as he has done.** Bear each other's burdens and so will you fulfil the Torah of Christ. If anybody thinks that he is something, he deceives himself because he is nothing. Let each person prove himself by his actions, then he can take pride in himself without comparing himself to anybody else. Each man must accept responsibility for himself.

Let him who is instructed in the word **of Christ** share his wealth with his teacher. Do not allow yourself to be led astray. God cannot be played with. What a man sows, so he will reap. The one who sows the desires of his flesh will reap decay but the one who sows the yearnings of the spirit will reap eternal life. Let us never be frustrated by the results of our good behaviour, for in its proper time we shall reap the **harvest of our righteousness,** so long as we persist. So, as we have the opportunity, let us do good to all people, and most of all to the family of believers. (See what large letters I use when I write in my own hand.)

Those who want to make a good external impression wish to

compel you to be circumcised. The only reason for doing this is to avoid being persecuted because of the cross of Christ.[1] And those being circumcised do not in fact observe the Torah but they want you to be circumcised that they may boast of **your submission to the Torah by** your external appearance. May I never boast of anything except in the cross of the Lord Jesus Christ through whom the world **of the flesh** has been crucified to me and I to the world. Neither circumcision nor non-circumcision **has any relevance –** but a new creation – **that the Son-of-God died for the sins of all human flesh that we might rise with him to the life of the spirit and to life eternal.** Peace and mercy to all those who walk according to this guiding principle, and on Israel – God's people.[2]

Finally, if everything I have said has not persuaded you, let no one trouble me, for I carry on my body the marks of Jesus.[3] The grace of our Lord Jesus Christ be with your spirit, brothers. Amen.

[1] The Christians were being persecuted by the Romans as a seditious sect, while the Jews were given the full privileges of religious freedom because of their numbers and influence. Those Christians who saw themselves as fully Jewish could escape victimisation by proving the extent of their Jewish identity, e.g. circumcision and obedience to the Torah. Paul's emphasis on Christ not as a living prophet/messiah but as the Son-of-God who died for human sin made Christianity a religion separate from Judaism – which enjoyed the protection of the Roman Emperor.
[2] The literal translation: The Israel of God. Paul's intent here is to say that, while he is teaching a new way from Judaism, he still wishes the well-being of the Jews who do not follow the way because they are God's people from whom Jesus came – interestingly a position only now accepted by the Vatican after some 2,000 years.
[3] Is Paul claiming that he has the stigmata of Christ on him, or that he is suffering from the results of floggings, on behalf of Christ? I think the latter to be the case.

Letters to the Romans

FROM:
Paul, a servant of Jesus Christ,
Summoned to be an apostle,
Dedicated to tell the good tidings from God, which
He previously promised through his prophets,
Recorded in the holy writings,
Regarding his son – in flesh of the descendants of David –
Declared the Son-of-God because of the power of
The divine spirit through the resurrection of the dead –
That is, Jesus Christ our Lord,
From whom, through his grace, I was made an apostle
To call unto all the nations for his name's sake
To the obedience that comes through faith.
You also are among those called to be believers in Jesus Christ.
TO:
All of you in Rome who are holy because God loves you.
Grace to you and peace from
God our father and our Lord Jesus Christ.

First, let me thank my God through Jesus Christ for you – because **the strength of** your faith is being reported throughout the world. God, my witness – he, whom I spiritually serve by teaching the good news of **the coming of** his son, is my witness how I never stop mentioning you in my prayers, pleading that, by the will of God, somehow at last I will make a happy journey to come to you. I long to see you that I may give you spiritual inspiration to strengthen you, and that we may encourage each other through the faith we both share.

Brothers, I do not wish you to be ignorant of how often I intended to come to you – but until now have been prevented – to harvest converts **in Rome** with you as I succeeded in doing among other Gentiles. I have an obligation to Hellenists and barbarians[1], both to the wise and to the foolish, so to the extent of the power within me I am most eager to preach the good news to you who are in Rome.

I am **not inhibited or** embarrassed about preaching the good news because it is the source of God's power to save every believer, first the Jews and then the Hellenists. This is the revelation of God's justice: faith leading to an even greater faith, for it has been written: "The upright man lives through his faith." [Habbakuk 2:4] God's anger is coming from heaven against godless and wicked men who suppress the truth in **the arrogance of** their wickedness. The knowledge of God is obvious to them, because God has revealed it to them. Since the creation of the world, his eternal power and divine nature, though invisible, is clearly manifest by his creativity, so that men **who ignore his instructions** have no excuse.

Even though they experienced God, they did not respect him nor thank him as God. Because of the futility of their philosophical theories, their undiscriminating minds were filled with darkness. Claiming wisdom, they were turned into fools. They exchanged the glory of an immortal God for representations of ephemeral and transient men, birds, four-footed animals and reptiles. So God allowed them to follow the desires of their hearts for sexual depravity by which they mutually degrade their own bodies. They exchanged divine truth for a lie. They worshipped and served creatures rather than the one who created them, he who is to be praised for ever **as the source of all our blessings**. Amen.

Therefore, God abandoned them to shameless lust. Even their wives practised unnatural union rather than natural sex. Their men also gave up natural relations with women and burnt with lust for each other. Men did unseemly things with other men and received the appropriate penalty for their sins. As they did not think it fit to acknowledge God, he surrendered them to their

[1] *Barbaros* is the Greek for foreigners. It is an insight into ancient and perhaps even modern psychology that foreigners were perceived as barbarians, according to present usage. But to whom is Paul referring, if he means "foreigners"? He cannot mean the Jews, because he is one of them. He must be referring to our European ancestors. This indicates the extent of Paul's universalism.

depraved minds and reprobate behaviour. So they became satu-
rated with every type of wickedness, covetousness, evil, envy,
murder, violence, strife, treachery, malice, slander, gossip, God-
hatred, insolence, arrogance and boasting. They look for ways to
do evil – they are disobedient to parents, undiscriminating, faith-
less, heartless and without any pity. They know full well God's
righteous decree that those who do such things are worthy of
death; not only do they continue to behave in this manner, but
encourage others to do likewise.[1]

O man, **even you who do not approve the immoral practice of
others,** you have no excuse in judging others, for when you judge
them, you condemn yourself for you behave no differently. We
know that God's judgement is just. So do you think that when you
condemn those who practice such things, that you, **who do the
same wickedness,** will escape the judgement of God? Do you take
for granted his great kindness, his tolerance and long-suffering
patience without appreciating that the kindness of God is to
encourage repentance? Because of your stubbornness and lack of a
repenting heart, you store up for yourself anger in that day of
wrath – the day of the revelation of God's true justice. He will
requite each man according to his behaviour. Those who seek
fame, honour and immortality by constantly doing good, he will
reward with life eternal. To those self-serving individuals, who
reject the truth but follow the way of evil, there will be anger and
fury. Affliction and suffering will befall the life of every man who
persists in doing evil, first the Jews, **because they were the first to
receive God's teachings,** and then the Hellenists. But glory and
honour and peace will attend everyone who does good, Jews in the
first instance but Hellenists too, for God does not show favouritism.

All you who are under no obligation to the law **of Moses**[2] who

[1] Paul has the view, which I share, that however people behave, they know in their
hearts what is right and what is wrong.
[2] I have added **of Moses** to make sense of this passage. Everyone has norms and
standards for behaviour. Paul, as a Pharisaic Jew, must be making the point that
immorality will lead to the same punishment regardless of whether one is required
to keep the Jewish covenant or not. When Paul uses Law in this sense, I will
translate it as *Torah*, which are the laws found in the Five Books of Moses.

have sinned – you will perish, even though you had no obligation to the Torah. And all those who sinned according to the Torah will be judged by the Torah. For it is not those who hear the Torah who are identified with God but those who obey the Torah. For when Gentiles without the Torah behave by natural instinct in accordance with it, they become a law unto themselves, even without the benefit of the Torah, since they prove that the laws of the Torah are written in their hearts.[1] Their conscience acts as witness **to their behaviour;** their own thoughts will sometimes accuse them and sometimes defend them. This will be revealed on the day when, according to the good news I preach, God, through Jesus Christ, will judge the hidden places of men's hearts.

Now, if you are a Jew and have trust in the Torah and boast of your relationship to God, that you know his will and what is right because you are instructed by the Torah; which convinces you that you can be a guide to the **morally** blind and a light to those who walk in darkness, a teacher of the foolish and a tutor of infants, because the Torah is the embodiment of knowledge and truth – how is it then that you who teach others do not instruct yourself? You who preach against stealing, do you not steal? You who say that people should not commit adultery, do you not commit adultery? You who detest idols, do you not rob temples? You who boast about the Torah and then transgress it, do you not dishonour God? Because of you, the name of God is blasphemed among the Gentiles – so has it been written.[2]

Circumcision is indeed good if you keep the Torah, but if you transgress it, you become as if you had not been circumcised. Thus, if the uncircumcised keep the Torah's commandments, will they not be considered as circumcised? The one who is not circumcised physically, yet obeys the Torah, may condemn you

---

[1] I believe Paul's statement validates the previous footnote, for here he is quoting Moses" final speech to the Israelites: "The Torah is not in heaven . . . not across the seas . . . but in your mouth and heart to do it." [Deuteronomy 30:12-14]
[2] Isaiah 52:5. The context of this verse is to suggest that, as Israel is forced into exile because of her sins, God is blasphemed by the victors because he could not protect them.

who, though you have been circumcised and have the laws all written down, transgress the Torah. A man is not a Jew if he is only one externally or if his circumcision is merely physical. No, a man is a Jew, if he is one internally and his circumcision is the circumcision of the heart, which is of the spirit and not by the letter **of the** Torah.[1] Such a man's praise comes not from men but from God.

What then, **you may ask**, is the benefit of being a Jew and what is the value of circumcision? A great advantage in every way! First, because it was they who were entrusted with the very oracles of God. **You might say that, because they have not believed in Jesus, their Torah and circumcision is discredited.** What if some lacked faith! Will their lack of faith cancel God's loyalty **towards them**? Not at all. God is always true, though all men be false, as it is written **about God:** "You are just in your sentence and right in your judgements [Psalm 51:6]. But, if through our wickedness God is able to reveal his justice more convincingly, should we say, to use **foolish** human logic, that God is wrong in being angry with us? That is patently absurd! If this were the case how could God judge the world? Should someone still claim, "If my own falseness publicises God's truth and so increase his honour, why should I still be condemned as a sinner?" **If you argue this,** you could equally say as we are being slandered by those who maintain that we claim, "Let us do evil out of which good will come."[2] **Slandering us,** they deserve condemnation.

What shall we say, therefore? Are we any better **because we are Jews or because we are good Gentiles?** Not at all! Both Jews and Hellenists, as we previously said, are under the yoke of sin, as it is written:

"There is none who does good, not even one. [Psalm 14:3a]

"There is no man who understands. [Psalm 14:2b]

---

[1] Readers should note that Paul here uses the description of "Jew" in a very positive sense – further proof that, while he was revealing a radically different religion, he still considered himself as Jewish.

[2] That is, the end justifies the means.

"No person who is mindful of God.

All have turned bad, altogether foul. [Psalm 14:3]

"Their throat is an open grave, their tongue is slippery.
[Psalm 5:10]

"Viper's poison is on their lips. [Psalm 140:4]

"His mouth is full of oaths, deceit and fraud. [Psalm 10:7]

They hasten to shed the blood of the innocent,

Destructiveness and injury litter their paths.

"They do not care for the path of integrity. [Isaiah 59:7]

"There is no fear of God before his eyes." [Psalm 36:1]

Now we know, whatever the Torah says, it is intended for those **Jews** who are subject to it, but it is also meant to silence every mouth **by its justice** and to let the whole world know that they are under the judgement of God. But no one can declare themselves as righteous before him by observing the Torah **because no one can meet his standards.** The Torah's function is to make us conscious of what is sinful.

But, now, a truth from God, separate from the Torah, has been revealed to which both the Torah and the Prophets give witness, namely the justice of God through faith in Jesus Christ to all those who believe. There is no difference **between Jew and Hellenist, those who are subject to the Torah and those who are not,** for all have sinned and fall short of God's expectations, but are justified **and forgiven** by the free gift of gracious love – the redemption that comes through Jesus Christ. God made him an atonement for those who had faith in the divine sacrifice of his life.[1] By doing this, he revealed his great justice, because with forbearance he had allowed previous sins to go unpunished. He did this to reveal his **compassionate** justice at the present time by declaring as righteous those who believe in Jesus. So what now of our boastings **that we kept the Torah?** They are without substance. Of what law **that we obey** or of what **good** works **can we boast? Oh none of these** – no,

---

[1] The text says "blood". Blood as the "source" of life in the ancient view is identified with the life-force. For this reason the Torah forbids a person to eat animal flesh with its blood in it – for the blood was its "soul".

but only of the Torah[1] of faith **in Jesus.** For we maintain that a man is justified by faith separate from the observance of the Torah. Otherwise we would need to say that he is only the God of the Jews and not also of the Gentiles. But, yes, he is also the God of the Gentiles. There is one God who will declare as righteous both those who are circumcised with faith **in Christ** as well as the uncircumcised who share in that same faith. This does not mean that we nullify the Torah. It is not so. Indeed, we uphold the Torah, **but not without faith.**

In this regard, what can we learn from **the life of** Abraham, our biological ancestor? If Abraham was righteous through his works, he could well take pride in himself, but not with the assurance of God's approval. What do the writings say? "Abraham believed in God and this was why he was declared as righteous." [Genesis 15:6] **Consider,** when a man works, his wages are not given him as a favour but as his due, **but this does not entitle him to be reckoned as righteous before God.** When someone, however, who does not work, **that is, has no good deeds to his credit,** but believes in him who **with compassion** acquits the ungodly **from guilt,** his faith is considered as righteousness, **just as was Abraham's whether he did good or not.**

David is making the same point when he speaks of the happiness of the man whom God considers as righteous apart from **good** works: "Happy is he whose transgression is forgiven and whose sin is covered over. Happy is the man whom the LORD does not hold as guilty [Psalms 32:1-2]. Is this **divine reward of** happiness intended only for the circumcised **who are subject to the Torah** or also for the uncircumcised **who are not?** We have been talking about Abraham's faith as being ascribed to him as righteousness. When did this attribution take place? When he was circumcised or when he was uncircumcised? It was before he was

---

[1] The Greek text says *nomou pistos;* law of faith. As pointed out in a previous footnote, Paul means the Mosaic law – the Torah. The three-letter root of Torah is y-r-h which means "teaching". In modern Jewish translation of the Old Testament, Torah is translated as "Teachings".

circumcised! His circumcision, **therefore,** was a sign of the **divine** seal of righteousness he achieved by his faith while he was not yet circumcised **or subject to the Torah which had not yet been given.**

So, he is the **spiritual** father of all those who believe and are not uncircumcised and therefore considered to be among the righteous.[1] But he is also the **spiritual** father of the circumcised who are not only circumcised but who also walk in the faith of Abraham before he was circumcised.[2] **My point is that** it is not through the Torah that Abraham and his offspring were promised the world as their inheritance, but because of the righteousness that came from his faith. If keeping the Torah is all that is required to inherit the world, then faith is of no consequence and God's promise is without foundation. **Abraham's faith in him and not the Torah is the basis of God's promise to the descendants of Abraham that they would inherit the earth. Consider, Abraham acted righteously out of his faith.** The Torah leads to divine retribution, and where there is no Torah, there is no transgression, **that is to say that the Torah is only necessary because of the existence of transgression which comes from the lack of faith.**

The divine promise is the consequence of faith, so that it comes out of God's graciousness **as a gift** to all of Abraham's descendants, not only to those who are subject to the Torah, but to those also who share in Abraham's faith. He is the father of us all, as it is written, "I have made you a father of many nations." [Genesis 17:5] In the sight of God – Abraham is our father – the God in whom he believed, who gives life to the dead and summons into being that which did not exist.

He, **who because of his advanced age**, was beyond hope **of having children,** believed **in God's promise** and so became the father of many nations as he had been promised: **"Look toward heaven and count the stars and see if you are able to count them,**

[1] The Gentiles.
[2] The Jews.

so shall your offspring be" [Genesis 15:5].[1] Without any weakening of his faith **in God's promise**, he knew that in reality his body was already as good as dead, as he was about one hundred years old, and that Sarah's womb was also dead. But, because of the promise of God, he resisted the scepticism born out of reality, but was empowered **and vitalised** by his faith to give glory to God, being totally convinced that God had the power to fulfil his promise. This is why it was credited to him as **an act of great righteousness**. The words, "it was credited to him," were not meant for him alone but also for us, to whom God will credit righteousness – for us who believe in him who raised Jesus our Lord from the dead. He was delivered over to death because of our sins and was raised again to life to acquit us **of our sins because of our faith in him.**

So then, now that we have been justified by faith,[2] we have been reconciled to God through our Lord, Jesus Christ, through whom by our faith we have gained God's favour under **whose beneficence** we are living, and we rejoice in the hope of the revelation of God's glory, **when our Lord Jesus will return to us.** Not only this, but we rejoice in our sufferings because sufferings develop perseverance which develops character which leads to hope. And hope will not lead to disillusionment because God has poured out his love into our hearts through the divine spirit he has instilled into us.

While we were still helpless, the Anointed One – Christ – died for the wicked at the appointed time. **This was incredible** for who will even die on behalf of a just man? Perhaps for a very righteous person, one might sacrifice his life. But this is how God demonstrated

[1] I have inserted the entire verse which is not quoted in the original text. Paul would have assumed familiarity with this text which is strange as he is addressing a Gentile audience who would not know the Torah, or is this an indication that the Roman Christian community included Jews and that the Gentile converts to Jesus were expected to become familiar with the Five Books of Moses. It would seem so. Otherwise, what would be the force of his arguments from the Hebrew Scriptures? He is seeking to prove to Gentiles that they can become descendants of Abraham without being circumcised or subject to the Torah.

[2] Justification through faith implies the forgiveness of sin and the gift of eternal life in the presence of God. Modern usage of justification means to rationalise one's behaviour and to find excuses for it. Sometimes, therefore, I have used the term "acquittal from sin" as a more appropriate translation of "*dikaiosin*".

his love for us. While we were still sinners, Christ died for us. Now that we, **through our faith**, have been justified by his death **and resurrection**, how much more will we be saved through him from God's retribution **on the day of God's judgement!** For if, when we were God's enemies, we were reconciled to God through the death of his son, how much more, having been so reconciled, shall we be saved by his life. Not only is this so, but we continue to rejoice in God through our Lord, Jesus Christ, through whom we achieved our reconciliation **to God.**

As sin entered the world through one man**'s disobedience**, and death **entered the world** through that sin, death came to all humankind, since everyone sinned **because of him.** Even before the Torah was given, sin was already in the world. But sin is not reckoned when there is no Torah. Death, however, reigned from the time of Adam to the time of Moses for even those who did not, like Adam, sin by disobedience were deemed as sinful. Adam was **in this sense** the model of the One to Come. **For, if death have dominion over all mankind because of the sin of one man, Adam, will not eternal life come from the atonement of Jesus Christ?**

But unlike the sin **and punishment of Adam** is the free gift **of God's gracious forgiveness.** If by the offence of one man so many died, how much more would the grace of God and the gift of grace that came through one man – Jesus Christ – abound for the many **who believe in him who brings them forgiveness and eternal life.** Let me repeat this: the gift of God did not come as the consequence of one man's sin. The judgement followed one sin and led to the condemnation **of death,** but the gift **of God** followed many trans- gressions and brought justification **through faith.** For if, by the sin of one man, death was given dominion over the earth through that one man, how much more will those who receive in abun- dance the gracious gift of righteousness have the power of life through one man – Jesus Christ.

Just as one sin led to the condemnation of all, so also through the obedience of one man – all are acquitted **of their sin** and given the gift of life. Just as, through the obedience of one man, many were made sinners, so through the one righteous act – **the crucifixion –** will many become righteous. With the giving of the Torah, sins increased **because many laws could be broken.** But, when the possibility of sin increases, the grace **of forgiveness for these sins** increases even more. Just as sin brought the reign of death, so also **divine** grace may reign through righteousness to bring eternal life through Jesus Christ, our Lord.

"So too in his resurrection, we are united with him"

Shall we say then that we should go on sinning, so that **proof of the divine** grace **of forgiveness** should increase? Of course not. We died to sin **through Jesus" death**. How, therefore, shall we continue to live in sinfulness? Or do you not realise that whoever was baptised in **the belief in** Jesus Christ was baptised by his death. We were therefore buried with him through the baptism of death in order that, as the Anointed One – Christ – was raised from the dead by the glorious power of the father, so too were we to begin a new life **without sin and without death.** For if we were united with him in his death, so too in his resurrection are we united with him. We know that our old selves were crucified with him so that the body full of sin would be destroyed and that we would no longer be subject to sin – for anyone who has died is freed from sinfulness.

Now, if we believe that we died with Christ, we also believe that we live with him. We also know that the Messiah -once having been raised from the dead – can no longer die. Death has no more dominion over him. In his death to sin he died once and for all, and the life he now lives is for God. So too must you see that you are indeed dead to sinfulness but alive to God in Jesus Christ. Therefore, do not let sin have dominion over your mortal body so that you fall prey to its lustfulness. Nor should you offer the limbs of your body to sin to be the weapons for wickedness. Rather, present yourself to God, as one who has returned from death to live again and offer him your limbs as instruments for righteousness. For sin is no longer your master. You are no longer subject to the Torah **or**

its judgements but are the recipients of God's grace **and loving-kindness.**

Will you then conclude that we may sin because we are not subject to the Torah but under the protection of his grace? Of course not! Surely you know, when you volunteer to be someone's obedient slaves, you become slaves to your master – whether you are slaves to sin – which is death, or in case of obedience to God – to righteousness **and life eternal.** But thanks be to God that, as once you were the slaves of sin, you now obey with a full heart the teaching delivered to you. Consequently, you have been liberated from sin to which you used to be enslaved and have turned to righteousness.

I speak in human metaphors to point out the weakness of your flesh **to resist the mastery of sin over you.** Just as you used to offer your limbs as slaves to impurity and sinfulness, so now offer them as slaves to righteousness in order to sanctify yourselves. When you were slaves to sin you were devoid of righteousness. What benefits did you then enjoy? **Admit it** – things of which you are now ashamed. For the consequence of those things is death. But now, being freed from sin and enslaved to God, the benefits are your sanctification and the reward of eternal life. The wages of sin are death, but the free gift of God is life eternal in Jesus Christ our Lord.

Or are you ignorant, brothers – for I know that I speak to those who are learned in the Torah – of the fact that the Torah has authority over a man only so long as he lives, for example a married woman is tied to her husband by the Torah so long as he is alive. Once the husband died, she is released from her marital ties. Thus, while the husband is alive, she will be called an adulteress if she goes to another man. But, if her husband dies, she is released of the bond and is not an adulteress if she gets another husband. Likewise, my brothers, you were released from the Torah – you died to it through the body of Christ, so that you belonged – **were married** – to another one who had risen from the dead in order that we might bear the fruits **of righteousness** to God. While we lived under the mastery of the flesh, the Torah, **by its prohibitions,** incited our limbs to do the wicked things which bring death. But now, having died **to the sinfulness** that enslaved us, we are discharged from the Torah and are able to serve **God** with a new spirit rather than by traditional obedience to the written code.

Would you conclude then **from what I am saying** that the Torah is sin? Of course not. But, I would not have knowledge of sin except through the Torah. I would not have known what it was to covet if the Torah had not said, "You shall not covet . . ." [Exodus 20:17 and Deuteronomy 5:21]. But sin, seizing the opportunity of my awareness of the commandment, produced in me every kind of covetous desire.[1] Without Torah sin has no existence.[2] I was living without the Torah, but when the commandments were given sin revived in me and I died. The commandments which were intended to bring life brought death instead. Sin, taking advantage of the incitement aroused by the commandment, seduced me and put me to death. But still the Torah is divine and the commandment is divine, righteous and good.[3]

"I want to do good but I cannot"

Did that which was **in essence** good become death for me? Of course not. In order that sin might be recognised as sin, it produced death in me through what was good, **namely the laws of the Torah**, so that through the commandments sin revealed its

[1] This is one of Paul's strangest concepts. Most would think that the Ten Commandments were a reaction to human wrongdoings and not the cause for them.

[2] This is true to the extent that, in the absence of laws, all behaviour could be seen to be permitted. Literally the verse says: "Without Torah, sin is dead."

[3] Paul's argument reveals his belief in the perversity of human nature. Laws are good but incite people to evil because their response to moral commandments is to do the opposite. There is for Paul no middle ground between evil and innocence. Those who died to sin in Jesus and were reborn again to the life of the spirit need no laws. The law is within them. In the Torah, however, Moses states that the Torah is life, "I have put before you life and good and death and evil– choose life and live." [Deuteronomy 30:15-16] Paul's rejection of this view is a serious departure from Judaism and puts Christianity on an altogether different religious level. Paul's pessimism about human nature seems to be based on his own honest self-assessment which follows.

enormous sinful power. We know that the Torah is spiritual, but I am bound by the flesh and have been sold as a slave to sin. I do not understand why I do what I do. For I do not what I want to do but I do what I hate to do. And if I do what I do not want to do, I must agree that the Torah is good **and necessary**. But no matter, it is no longer I who am doing it, but the sin which dwells inside me. Nothing good dwells inside me because of my **sinful** flesh. I want to do good but I cannot, but the evil I do not want to do – I do. If, therefore, I do what I do not want to do, it is not I who do it, but the sin that dwells within me.

So, this is the "law" I have discovered – that, even when I want to do good, the desire for evil is always present. I delight in God's Torah in my inmost being, but there is a different law in my limbs warring against the law of my mind which takes me captive to the law of sin which is working in the limbs of my flesh. I am a wretched man. Who will deliver me from this body of death? Thanks be to God – through Jesus Christ our Lord. **Only through him am I delivered.** So then, as for myself, my mind is subject to the Torah of God, but my flesh is subject to the law of sin.

Now, therefore, there is no condemning judgement for those who are united with Jesus Christ, because, through him, the spiritual law of life freed me from the law of sin and **its consequence which is** death. For the Torah was powerless because of the weakness of the flesh. Therefore, God sent his own son in the form of sinful flesh and in that body God condemned sin. **So he died in the flesh to sin and was resurrected to the life of the divine spirit.** This was so that the proper demands of the Torah might be met by us who do not walk according to the flesh but according to the spirit.[1] Those who live according to the flesh set their mind on the things of the flesh, but those who live according to the spirit set their minds on things of the spirit. The mind-set of the flesh leads to death, but the mind-set of the spirit leads to life and contentment.

---

[1] *Pneuma*, translated as spirit, must refer to the inspiration in man of the divine spirit. It is obvious but well to keep in mind that "being in Christ" meant living with the mystical sense of having the divine spirit within one as God's gift for believing in the mystery of Christ on the cross. See what follows.

As the mind of sinful flesh is hostile to God, it will not submit itself to the Torah of God, nor indeed can it. Those who are entrapped by the desires of their flesh cannot find favour with God.

You, however, live not in the flesh but in the spirit because the spirit of God lives in you. If you did not have the spirit of Christ in you, you would not belong to him. But if the Christ is in you, your body is dead to sin but your spirit is alive to righteousness. If the spirit of the one who raised Jesus from the dead is in you, that same one who raised the dead Jesus Christ will also give **eternal** life to your own mortal bodies through his spirit who lives in you.

So then, brothers, we are under no obligation to the flesh or to live according to the dictates of the flesh. If you live for the flesh, you will die, but if by the power of the **divine** spirit you kill the wicked activities of the body, you will live. Those who are led by the spirit of God are the sons of God. The **divine** spirit you received is not a servile spirit based on fear **of God** but the **loving paternal** spirit which makes you his sons. **When we speak to him, we do not call him master** but we say, "Abba[1], father." The divine spirit itself and our spirit both give witness that we are children of God. And if children, we are also heirs – heirs of God jointly with Christ since we suffer with him so that we may also share in his glory. I believe that the sufferings we endure presently are not to be compared to the measure of the coming glory which is to be revealed to us. **All of** creation is eagerly waiting for him to reveal **whom he has chosen as** the son of God.

The world was ruled by futility not of its own choice but by the will of the one who is its ruler in the hope that the whole creation would liberate itself from the process of decay to enjoy the freedom of the glory of being the children of God. For we know that all of creation has **for years without number** been groaning with the pangs of childbirth until now. Not only is this so, but we ourselves, we who are the first fruit of the spirit, have been groaning in anticipation of the redemption of our bodies and in anticipation of our adoption as children of God. By hope **in the fulfilment of this** were

[1] Meaning father in Hebrew and Aramaic.

we saved. But hope which is seen, **that is to say it is guaranteed to happen,** is not hope **but reality**. Who hopes for what he already has? But, if we hope for what we do not have, we wait for its realisation with patience.

Likewise, the divine spirit helps us in our limitations. **For example,** if we do not know how to pray, the divine spirit itself through our speechless groans makes supplications on our behalf, for the one who searches the **human** heart knows the intention of our spirit because the divine spirit intercedes for his holy ones as this is the will of God. We know that in all matters God works for the good of those who love him and who have been chosen according-ing to his purpose **for them.** He had described beforehand who were destined to be like his son his first-born among many brothers. And those whom he preordained to be called, he also declared as righteous and to those whom he declared as righteous, he also gave of his glory.

What then shall we say of these things? If God is before us, who can prevail against us? He who did not spare his own son but deliv-ered him **for crucifixion** for our sake, will he not now then, along with him, graciously give us all his blessings? Who will bring a charge against God's chosen ones? If God declares who are right-eous, who is to condemn **them**? Jesus Christ who died but was raised **to life** and is at God's right hand – he pleads for us. Who is there who can separate us from the love of Christ! Neither afflic-tion, nor distress, nor persecution, nor famine, nor nakedness, nor any peril, nor war **will separate us from him**, as it is written, "For your sake we confront death the whole day long. We are reckoned as sheep ready to be slaughtered." [Psalm 44:22] No, in all these matters we are even greater than conquerors through **the power of** him who loves us. For I am convinced that neither death nor life, nor Messengers of God, nor rulers, nor things present or yet to come, nor powers residing in heights or the depths, nor anything else in all of creation will prevent us from loving God through Jesus Christ our Lord.

I speak truthfully in the **spirit of** Christ. I do not lie. My con-science inspired by the divine spirit is witness to how grieved I am and to my unending heartache. I would that I myself were accursed and separated from our Messiah – Christ – for the sake of my own brothers who are of my own stock, those who are **born** Israelites. They were adopted by God as sons. Theirs is the glory of the covenants **with God**, the receipt of the Torah, the Temple worship and the promises **for their triumphant future.** Theirs also are the patriarchs; and from them through his physical being, comes the Messiah who is over all. God be forever praised, Amen! **But they have rejected him.**

This does not mean that God fails to keep his promise **to deliver the Israelites. Consider,** not all those who are descended from Israel[1] are to be considered as Israelites. **This is no different from the situation of Abraham's descendants.** Being of the seed does not make them all his children. The opposite is proven **when God says to Abraham when he is distressed by the exile of his first-born son Ishmael,** "Through Isaac shall your descendants bear your name" [Genesis 21:12]. This is to indicate that it is not physical descendants who are God's children but it is the children **who will enjoy the fulfilment** of the promise **first given through Abraham, then through Christ,** who are regarded as Abraham's descendants. The words of the promise were: "At this season next year I will return and Sarah will have a son" [Genesis 18:10,14].

Even more to the point: Rebecca who conceived **twins** to Isaac our ancestor – even before they were born and had the chance to do good or evil, in order that God's chosen purpose should be fulfilled, not on the basis of deeds, but on whom he elected, she was told, "The older shall serve the younger" [Genesis 25:23]. **This was later confirmed by the prophet,** "Jacob I loved, but Esau I hated"[2] [Malachi 1:2,3]. What shall we say then, that God is unjust? Speaking to Moses he says, "I will have mercy on whomever I have mercy and I will have compassion on whom I have compassion" [Exodus 33:19]. So, it does not depend on human will or effort, but

---

[1] The other name for Jacob, the ancestor of the twelve tribes of Israel.

[2] This does not satisfactorily defend God against the accusation of injustice. Where is the fairness of being chosen or rejected even before one's birth? The following verse confirms God's arbitrary right to be "gracious" to whomever he pleases.

on God's grace. Indeed it is written that God says to Pharaoh: "For this very reason, I have allowed you to survive – to show off my power so that the story of my fame will spread throughout all the earth" [Exodus 9:16]. So we see that God shows mercy to whom he wants and hardens the hearts of those he wants to harden.

"Who are you to remonstrate with God?"

But you, therefore, will say to me, "How can God find fault with anyone, if no one can resist his will?" But who are you to remonstrate with God? Does that which is created say to its creator, "Why did you make me this way?" Does not the potter have the right to make out of one lump of clay objects to be used for special and vulgar purposes? What if God, wanting to show his anger and to display his power, **decides to delay taking action** and therefore shows great patience for a time towards those sentenced to destruction. Suppose he did this to reveal the extent of his glory to the persons on whom he had mercy, whom he had already pre-ordained to honour, namely us whom he elected not only from among the Jews but also from among the Gentiles, as he says in Hosea: "Those who were not my people I will call my people and she who was not beloved I will call beloved"[1] and "In every place where it was said to them, "You are not my people, there they shall be called: sons of the living God'" [Hosea 1:10].

Isaiah cries out concerning Israel, "For though your people Israel were as numerous as the sand of the sea, only a remnant will be saved, for the Lord will carry out his sentence quickly and decisively against the earth" [Isaiah 10:22,23].[2] It is as Isaiah had previously stated, "Unless the Lord of Hosts had left us descendants we would have become like Sodom and made like Gemorrah" [Isaiah 1:9]. What shall we then say, that Gentiles who did not pursue righteousness **by observing the Torah** have obtained it – the righteousness that comes through faith; and that Israel, who

---

[1] This proof text is an interpretative translation of Hosea 2:23.

[2] Paul seems to be quoting a variant text or paraphrasing it to suit his argument.

pursued the Torah of righteousness, did not succeed in fulfilling the law? Why did they fail? Because their efforts were not based on faith but on the basis of deeds. They tripped over the stumbling stone, as it is written, "See, I am laying a stone in Zion that will make people stumble, a rock that will make them fall, but the one who trusts in him will never be put to shame!"[1] [Isaiah 8:14; 28:16].

Brothers, my heart's desire and my prayer to God is for them, **the Israelites** that they be saved. I am witness to their zeal for God, but it is not enlightened **by faith in Jesus.** Unaware that righteousness comes **as a gift** from God, they tried to establish their own righteousness **on the basis of keeping the Torah,** they did not submit to God's righteousness **which is given through faith in the Anointed Jesus.** Christ is the fulfilment of the Torah so that righteousness may be attained for everyone who believes **in him.** Moses writes about the righteousness that comes from obeying the Torah: "Whoever keeps them will have life through them" [Leviticus 18:5]. But the righteousness that comes through faith says, "Do not ask in your heart who will ascend in heaven (that is, to bring Christ down) or who will descend into the abyss (that is to bring Christ up from the dead)?" But what does the text say, "The word is near to you. It is in your mouth and heart" [Deuteronomy 30:12-14].[2] This is the word of faith we proclaim. Because, if you confess with your mouth the Lord Jesus and believe in your heart that God raised him from the dead, you will be saved **for eternal life.** For with **faith in** the heart you are led to righteousness and the confession of the mouth leads to salvation. As the Writings say, "He who believes in him will not be put to shame" [Isaiah 28:16].[3]

[1] This quotation only resembles the actual texts from Isaiah. What Paul is saying is that the Torah became a stumbling block but that the faith in Jesus is the foundation stone of righteousness which is utterly reliable.

[2] Paul, to prove his point, takes liberties with the text. Moses is speaking of "the commandment" when he says that "it is in your mouth and heart to observe it." Paul omits, "to observe it". Also, in the text Moses does not ask, "Who will descend into the abyss," but rather, "who will cross the seas to fetch it?" The words in parenthesis are Paul's interpretation of the text's meaning.

[3] Paul paraphrases the text which does not refer to any person but to a prophecy.

There is no difference between Jew and Hellenist. The same Lord is over all, richly blessing all who call on him. "Everyone who calls on the name of the Lord will be saved" [Joel 2:32]. But how can they call on one in whom they do not believe? And how may they believe in the one whom they have not heard? And how can they hear without someone to tell them the **good** news? And how can they tell the good news if they are not sent? As it has been written, "How beautiful are the feet of those who bring good news!" [Isaiah 52:7]. But not all believed the good news. Isaiah also says: "Lord, who believed what they heard from us?" [Isaiah 52:7]. Faith, then, comes from hearing **the good news,** and the message we are talking about is the word of Christ.

But then I must ask: did they not hear? Yes, **they did, as it is written in the Psalms:** "Yet their report goes out throughout the earth, and their words to the end of the world" [19:4]. But, I ask again: "Did Israel not know?" First Moses says, "I will rouse them to jealousy with a "no-people". I will provoke you with a foolish nation" [Deuteronomy 32:21].[1] Then Isaiah boldly states: "I was found by those who did not seek me. I revealed myself to those who did not ask for me, **that is the Gentiles.**[2] [Isaiah 65:1] But, in regard to Israel, he says, "All day long, I stretched out my hands to a disobedient and obstinate people" [65:2].

I ask then, does this mean that God has rejected his people? Not at all. Even I am an Israelite, of the descendants of Abraham from the tribe of Benjamin.[3] God did not reject his people whom he had known before **they became a nation.** Know you not how the writings in a passage describe Elijah's appeal to God against the Israelites: "Lord, they have killed your prophets; they have dug up your altars. I am the only one left and they also seek my

---

[1] The preceding verses give the context of Paul's argument against the Jews. Moses warns the Israelites that, as a consequence of their worship of "no-gods", a "no-people" will inspire their envy – the Gentiles who replaced them in God's favour because they believed in Jesus.

[2] This is not an exact translation of the traditional texts.

[3] This claim is interesting as King Saul, (and Saul is Paul's original name) was from the tribe of Benjamin.

life" [I Kings 19:10,14]. What was God's reply to him? "I have left for myself seven thousand who have not bowed the knee to Baal" [I Kings 19:18]. So too, even now, there is a remnant chosen by grace. If by grace, then it is no longer a matter of works, **namely obedience to the decrees of the Torah.** If it were through works **that they were chosen** then grace would not be grace, **because it would not be the way towards righteousness and eternal life.**

What then? Israel did not obtain what it was seeking, but those chosen **by grace** obtained it. The rest **of them who had been rejected** were hardened, as it is written:[1] "God has dulled their senses, eyes that could not see and ears that could not hear to this very day" [Deuteronomy 29:4]. And David says, "Let their table become a snare and a trap [an offence and retribution for them]. Let their eyes be darkened so that they cannot see and their backs always bent over" [Psalm 69:22-23].[2] I ask, therefore, when they stumbled was their fall permanent? Not at all. By their trespass, salvation came to the Gentiles which provoked their jealousy. Now, if their trespass enriched the world and their defects meant riches for the Gentiles, how much more will their full inclusion bring? **Because they rejected Jesus as the Messiah the apostles turned to the Gentiles and more were saved. Praise be to God.**

I am talking to you Gentiles because I am indeed the apostle to the Gentiles. I am proud of my mission **to the Gentiles** in the hope that I will provoke the jealousy of my own flesh **and blood so that they will join you** and thus save some of them. If their rejection **of Christ** led to the reconciliation of the world **through him because otherwise we may not have turned to the Gentiles,** their re-acceptance **of him** will be like the resurrection of the dead. If the first part of the dough offered as the first fruits is **set aside as**

---

[1] This suggests that God purposely hardened their hearts, as he had done to Pharaoh. Does this not place full responsibility for human behaviour on God's will? This leads to the rabbinic paradox: All is pre-ordained, but humanity has free will.
[2] The phrase in parenthesis is not to be found in the traditional text. Could it be that Paul was working with a different text from that which has come down to us?

holy,[1] is not the whole loaf holy and if the roots **and trunks** of trees are holy, are not the branches also holy?

Now, if some branches **of an olive tree** have been broken off, **that is those Jews who have rejected Jesus,** and you, who **as Gentiles,** like a wild olive shoot grafted among the other branches, **[that is those Jews who accepted Christ]** take nourishment from the richness of the roots of the olive tree, do not consider yourselves as superior to the other branches **that broke off, namely, the Jews.** And if you do feel superior, **just remember that** you do not maintain the Jewish roots, they maintain you. **Of course,** you could very well say, "The branches were broken off so that I might be grafted in." True, but they were broken off **not by God's will** but by their unbelief and you are there **[grafted in]** because of your faith. Do not be arrogant but stand in reverential awe. If God did not spare the natural branches, **the children of Israel,** he might also not spare you **if you too become arrogant.**

Rather, consider **this as an example of both** the kindness and severity of God: severity to those **branches** which fell; on the other hand, the kindness of God towards you, but only if you deserve his kindness – otherwise you too, **like the unfaithful Israelites,** could be cut off. But, if they do not persist in their disbelief, they will be grafted back in among the branches. For if you who were cut out of an olive tree that was wild by nature and contrary to nature still were grafted into a cultivated olive tree, how much more easily will these, the natural branches, be grafted into their own olive tree?

Brothers, I do not want you to be ignorant of this mystery lest you take pride in your own wisdom **in choosing Christ.** The hardness that has happened to part of Israel is only until the full number of Gentiles has come in, in order that **eventually** all Israel will be saved as it is written:

---

[1] The true meaning of holy is often lost. It means more than spiritual or symbolic of the divine. It has the force of something which has been set aside or dedicated to God. Thus the first fruits are dedicated to God, and a holy man is one who dedicates himself exclusively to serving God.

"The deliverer will come out of Zion
He will turn godlessness from Jacob
This is my covenant with them
When I take away their sins."[1]

In so far as the good news **we bring, because they reject it** they are enemies. But you enjoy the benefit **in their rejection.** As far as election is concerned, they are **still** beloved **and chosen** because of their patriarchs,[2] for God never repents of his free gifts **of grace** to those whom he has called. Just as you, who were in the past disobedient to God, have now received mercy because of their disobedience, **in so far as had they not become broken branches you could not have been grafted onto their tree.** In the same way, while they are now disobedient, through the mercy shown to you, they will also obtain mercy. God has bound all people to disobedience so that he may show mercy to them all.

"Oh, the depth of riches and the wisdom and knowledge of God
How inscrutable are his judgements
And how unsearchable his ways?
Who can know the mind of the Lord
Who can become his counsellor?
Who has ever given to God that God should repay him?
Because of him and through him do all things come.
To him be glory forever. Amen."

I urge you, therefore, by God's mercy, to make your bodies living sacrifices dedicated and acceptable to God – that is to say your spiritual worship. Do not conform any longer to the fashions of the age

---

[1] Quotation based on Isaiah 59:20 and 27:9. This is a fascinating exoneration of the Jews who rejected Christ. This was God's will so that Paul was permitted to engage in an outreach programme which could lead to universal salvation. Had all the Jews accepted Christ, they would have maintained a parochial and exclusivistic attitude. In fact the Pharisees were missionaries to the Gentiles. Jesus attacks them for it: "You travel over land and sea to make a simple convert [Matthew 23:15]. Jesus says that his mission is only to the lost sheep of Israel: see Matthew 10:61: "Go rather to the lost sheep of Israel" or 15:24: "I am not sent but to the lost sheep of Israel.'

[2] Descendants benefiting on the basis of *Zechut Avot*, the "merit of the Patriarchs", is an ancient rabbinic concept and principle.

but transform yourself by rethinking your ideas, so that you may discover the will of God – that which is good, pleasing, indeed perfect. I say to you by the grace given to me to each of you, do not think yourself as more superior than you are; rather judge yourself objectively, in relationship to the amount of faith God has allotted to you. As each of us has one body with many limbs each with different functions, so do we in Christ form one body, each belonging to the others, but having different gifts according to the grace bestowed upon us. If a man's gift is prophecy, let him use it but to the extent of the amount of his faith; or if it is **the gift of** practical service, let him be an administrator; or if it is that of moral exhortation, let him preach; or if it is that of philanthropy, let him be generous; or of skills of leadership, let him be conscientious; or if it is the gift of showing compassion, let him do it with a cheerful disposition.

Let love be genuine. Avoid what is evil and clasp at opportunities for doing good. With brotherly love, love each other with warmth. Respect others more than yourself. Do not lose your enthusiasm. Be spiritually passionate in your service of the Lord. Rejoice in hope. Endure affliction. Pray regularly, contribute to the needs of the pious. Seek opportunities to be hospitable. Ask God's blessing on those who persecute you. Do not curse but bless them. Rejoice with those who rejoice. Weep with those who weep. Be mindful of each other's needs. Do not be aloof but mix with ordinary people. Do not consider yourself as wise. Do not repay evil with evil. Behave in such a way as to win universal approval. And, insofar as it rests with you, seek to be at peace with everyone. My dear friends, do not seek to avenge yourselves but leave room for the wrath **of the day of God's judgement** to come, as it is written, "Vengeance is mine, I will pay them back," says the LORD [Deuteronomy 32:35]. Rather, "If your enemy is hungry, feed him, if he is thirsty, give him drink. By this you will be piling red-hot coals on his head."[1] [Proverbs 25:21-22]

---

[1] Your kindness will make his ultimate punishment even greater, because his behaviour will compare unfavourably with yours.

Do not let evil become your master but defeat evil with goodness.

Let everyone subject themselves to the authority of the government, for all authority comes from God. The existing authorities have been ordained by God. Thus he who resists authority is rebelling against God's institutions. Those who do this will bring judgement against themselves. For rulers do not cause fear to those who behave properly but only to those who do wrong.[1] If you want to be free of anxiety before authority, behave properly and you will win its praise. It is God's agent for your own protection. But, if you behave improperly, be anxious for he does not wield power for nothing. He is God's agent to execute the wrath of judgement on the wrongdoer. It is, therefore, necessary to submit to authority not only out of fear of punishment but also because of conscience. You pay taxes for the same reason. They are agents of God who are working full time. Pay to everyone what is due to them – taxes to whom taxes are due, income to whom income is due, respect to whom respect is due and honour to whom honour is due.

"Love is the fulfilment of the Torah"

Let no debt remain unpaid except the debt to love one another for he who loves the other has fulfilled the Torah. **The commandments:** You shall not commit adultery, you shall not kill, you shall not steal, you shall not covet and whatever other commandments are summed up in this command: You shall love your neighbour as yourself. Love does not allow one to harm one's neighbour. Love is, therefore, the fulfilment of the Torah. For you know that the time of **judgement** has come. It is the moment to rise out of your slumber, for **the time of** our salvation is closer than it was when we first believed. The night is passing and the day is drawing near. Let us, therefore, cast off the works of darkness and put on

---

[1] A rather naïve view of rulers' beneficence,all the more amazing as Paul lived in the days of the despotic Roman emperors and their sycophants. He must be expressing a general concept of respect for authority.

the armour of light. Let us behave properly as we would in broad daylight, **when all is seen**, with no riotous revelling, no drunkenness, no promiscuity or debauchery, nor in quarrels or jealousies. Rather, clothe yourself with the Lord Jesus Christ and do not think of how to gratify the lustfulness of your flesh.

Welcome those with an uncertain faith but not in order to judge them on varying ideas **as to how one should live as a member of our community.** One person of **strong** faith may have no inhibitions about eating everything; yet another person of uncertain faith may limit himself to vegetables.[1] The person who eats everything should not despise the vegetarian, nor should the vegetarian sit in judgement on the other person, for God accepts them **all.** Who are you to condemn the servant of someone else's household? It is only before his master that he stands or falls. And if he is able to stand erect it is because this is in his master's power.

Also, there are those who make a distinction between the importance of one day over another and those who treat all days as equal. **What is important is that** each person should act out of his personal conviction; so long as he observes a day **as special** he does so to honour the Lord. Equally, so too the man who eats everything eats in honour of the Lord for he gives thanks to God **for the food he has eaten,** and he who abstains does so for the Lord, for he also gives thanks to God **for what he has eaten.** None of us live for ourselves alone, nor does one die to oneself alone. If we live we live for the Lord and when we die we die for the Lord. So, whether we live or die, we are the Lord's. For this reason did Christ die and lived again so that, over both the living and dead, he would be the Lord.

This being so, why do you judge or even despise your brother,

---

[1] The importance of this issue can only be appreciated in the context of the importance of keeping the dietary laws prescribed by Moses. In Acts, Peter and Paul both permit Gentile converts to eat all foods, "except meat sacrificed to pagan gods and improperly slaughtered animals which still contain their blood" [15:20]. Undoubtedly, however, the Jewish Christians would have kept the dietary laws and would have encouraged the Gentile Christians to do the same. One can appreciate that, as the original Christians lived in communities, they would often have communal meals and the differing eating habits could have caused friction.

for all of us will stand before the seat of God's judgement. As it has been written, "As I live says the Lord, every knee will bend down before me; every tongue will confess to God" [Isaiah 45:23]. Therefore, each one of us must make our own account before God. Let us not judge one another. Instead, agree not to place in your brother's way any obstacle to make him fall. **As for the matter of foods of which I was speaking,** I am convinced by **the teachings of** the Lord Jesus that nothing in itself is unclean.[1] But if a person considers it unclean, then it becomes unclean **for him**. If your brother is distressed by the food you eat, you are not acting in love **towards him if you eat such food in his presence.** Do not by what you eat cause the **spiritual** destruction of someone for whom Christ died. Do not let the goodness **of your Christian life** be reviled **because of what you eat. That would be a great pity** for the Kingdom of God is not about what one eats or drinks, but it is about righteousness, harmony and joy through the divine spirit; because only by serving Christ in this manner does one win the approval of God and man.

Therefore, we must pursue that which leads to harmonious relationships which give strength to each other. Do not for the sake of food undo all the efforts of God **for human salvation. In my view,** all foods are indeed permitted but it is still wrong to allow the offence of eating "offensive" food to lead others to fall away **from the faith in Jesus Christ.** Better not to eat meat or drink wine or anything which causes your brother to fall. Hold on to your beliefs **about what you may eat,** but keep them private to God. Praiseworthy is the person who does not bring a bad judgement upon himself by behaving according to what he believes is "right". But the man who is uncertain about what food is forbidden is condemned if he still eats it, because he eats not out of the conviction of his faith – and everything which does not come from faith is sinful.

We who are strong in our convictions should tolerate the

---

[1] Could Paul be referring to what Jesus is reported to have said in Matthew 15:10? "What goes into the mouth does not make anyone unclean; it is what comes out of the mouth that makes someone unclean.'

failings of the weak and not please ourselves **by proving our superiority.** Each of us should **by his behaviour** please his neighbour for the good purpose of building him up **in his faith.** For even Christ did not act to please himself, as it is written, "The reproaches of those who reproached you fall on me" [Psalm 69:9]. All that was written in the past was for our own instruction so that through our comfort in reading the Scriptures we might receive enduring hope. May the God who grants us the gift of patience and comfort grant you the gift of being in harmony with each other's thoughts in regard to Christ, so that you with one voice praise God and the father of our Lord Jesus Christ.

Wherefore accept one another as Christ accepted us to bring glory to God. For I say that Christ became a servant of the Jews on behalf of the truth of God to confirm the promises made to the patriarchs so that the Gentiles might praise God in his mercy, as it is written:

"For this reason I will extol you among the nations

I will sing praises to your name" [Psalm 18:49].

Again it says:

Rejoice O nations with his people" [Deuteronomy 32:43].

And again,

"Praise the LORD all you nations

And sing praises to him, all you peoples" [Psalm 117:1].

And again, Isaiah says,

"The root of Jesse will spring up

One who will rise up to rule the nations

One on whom the Gentiles will hope" [Isaiah 11:10].[1]

May the god of hope fill you all with joy and peace in believing so that you may abound in hope through the power of the divine spirit **within you.**

I am persuaded, my brothers, that you yourselves are also full of goodness being filled with knowledge and able to exhort one another. But I have written to you quite bluntly on some points to

---

[1] This is not an exact following of the traditional text. *Gens* is the Latin for nation (in Greek *ethnay*) hence: Gentiles.

reinforce them, by the grace granted to me by God that I should be the minister of Jesus Christ to the Gentiles dedicated to proclaiming the good news of God so that the Gentiles, sanctified by the divine spirit, would become an acceptable offering to God. I can therefore be proud through Jesus Christ in my work for God. I would not think of speaking of anything excepting what Christ has done through me to make Gentiles subject to him, by my example or teachings, by the execution of signs and wonders **granted me** by the power of the divine spirit; so that I fully proclaimed the good news of Christ from Jerusalem doing the rounds as far as Illyricum.

My mission to proclaim the good news was to places where the name of Christ was unknown, not to build on the foundations laid by other teachers, but as it is written, "Those who have not been told shall see and those who have not heard will comprehend" [Isaiah 52:15]. This is the reason why I was prevented from coming to you. But now as I am no longer needed in those regions and have had the desire over many years to see you, I plan to do so on my way to Spain. On this journey I look forward to seeing you and to be sent on by you **to complete my journey** once I have enjoyed your company for a little while. Now, however, I am going to Jerusalem to serve the needs of the holy ones there. For the holy communities of Macedonia and Achaia thought it proper for them to make some contribution to help the poor among the pious in Jerusalem. They thought this proper, and indeed they owe it to them for, if the Gentiles have shared in their – the Jews – spiritual blessings, they ought to reciprocate by sharing with them their material blessings.

So, after I have fulfilled this objective and made sure that they have received these contributions, I will pass through Rome on the way to Spain. I know that when I come to you, I will come with the fullness of Christ's blessings. I ask you my brothers, through our Lord Jesus Christ and through the love of the divine spirit to join me in my struggle **against those who do not believe** by praying to God on my behalf – so that I may be delivered from the disbelievers in Judea and that my ministry in Jerusalem be acceptable to the pious people there; so that I may by God's will joyously come to you and relax in your company. The God of peace be with you all. Amen.

I commend to you our sister, Phoebe, who also ministers to the community in Cenchrea. By the Lord receive her warmly as you would any of the holy ones, and give her any help that she may require from you because she has been a great support to many, including myself. Also, give greetings to Priscilla and Aquila, my fellow workers in Jesus Christ because they risked their necks to save my life. Not only I, but all the holy communities of the Gentiles are grateful to them.[1]

I implore you, brothers, to keep guard against those who cause divisions and offence against the teachings you have learnt. Keep away from them. Such men do not serve our Lord Christ but their own **greedy** bellies; through clever speeches and flattery they deceive the minds of the innocent. And while your faithfulness is known to all, over which I rejoice with you, I want you to be perceptive of goodness and innocent of that which is evil. Then will the God of peace crush Satan under your feet.

Now to him who can make you stand firm through the good news **I preach** and my proclamation of Jesus Christ according to the revelation of the mystery which has been secret for time eternal and which only now is disclosed through the prophetic writings by command of the eternal God, and made known to all the Gentiles to being about the obedience which comes out of faith – to the only God of wisdom render glory through Jesus Christ for all ages. Amen.

---

[1] A number of greetings follow which may be found in the appendix – Romans 16:5–16; 21–24.

Letter to the Philippians

FROM: *Paul and Timothy, servants of Jesus Christ*
TO: *All the holy ones in Jesus Christ at Philippi
together with the presiding elders and deacons.*

Grace and peace to you from God our father and the Lord Jesus Christ. I give thanks to my God every time I think of you. Whenever I pray for you, I pray with joy because of your acceptance of the good news from the first until now, confident that he who began the good work with you will complete it until the day of Jesus Christ. It is right for me to think of all of you in this way because I have you in my hearts, for whether in chains or in defending or confirming the good news – you all participate in God's grace **which has been given** to me. God is my witness how I long for all of you with the affection of Jesus Christ. I pray for this that your love may increase to fuller knowledge and deeper insight so that you may discern what really matters so that **through your behaviour** you will be pure and innocent in the day of Christ, filled with the fruit of righteousness through Jesus Christ to the glory and praise of God.

Now, I want you to know, brothers, that my situation has in fact advanced the spread of the good news. It has become known throughout the Praetorian Guard[1] and to everyone else that my imprisonment is for the sake of Christ. Because of my imprisonment, most of the brothers have been inspired to speak the word of God with greater daring and courage. While it is true that some are proclaiming Christ out of competitive envy **of me**, others do so with good intentions. The latter out of love, because they know that it is because of my defence of the good news that I am here in prison. The others proclaim Christ not sincerely but in opposition, hoping thus to make things worse for me while I am in prison.

[1] Paul is a prisoner in Rome. Apparently, he was moved from house arrest as recorded in Acts to imprisonment in the Imperial Palace.

What does it matter? What is important is that for whatever reason, whether insincerely or truthfully, Christ is being proclaimed and I rejoice in this. Yes, I will also rejoice for I know that through your prayers and my own line to the spirit of Jesus Christ, my situation will result in my salvation. With eager anticipation I hope that I will not be shamed, but with the courage I have always shown until now, Christ will be exalted in my flesh whether by my death or by my life. For me, to live is Christ and even to die would be a profit **for me.** If I continue to live in the flesh, I will enjoy the fruit of my labour **for Christ.** I am in conflict as what to choose. I am torn between the two. There is the desire to part **from this life** and to be with Christ, for this would be much better, but to remain alive in the flesh is more important for your sake. Convinced of this, I know that I will remain with you for your progress and joy in the faith, so that through my being with you, your pride in Christ will overflow because of me.

Whatever happens, behave in a manner worthy of the good news of Christ, so that whether I come to see you or am absent, I hear that you are standing firm in one spirit and as one body and soul striving together for the faith in the good news – not being in terror of those who oppose you, which will result in their destruction and your salvation. This is **the ordinance** of God because it was given to you for the sake of Christ, not only to believe in him but to suffer for his sake – the same struggle you saw me endure and now hear that I still have to bear.

If there is any encouragement in Christ, any solace in love, any fellowship in the spirit, any compassion and sympathy, make my joy complete by being of one mind, one love, one soul and one purpose. Do nothing out of selfishness or vainglory. Rather with humility act as though others are better than yourselves. Look not at your own interests alone but also at the interests of others. Trust one another with the same spirit that you feel in Jesus Christ, who while sharing the essence of God did not claim equality with God; he emptied himself **of his divinity** and made himself as if a slave, taking on a human likeness. Appearing as a man, he made himself even more humble to the point of submitting to death – the death of the cross. Therefore, God greatly exalted him and gave him greater renown than any other, so that at the hearing of the name of Jesus, every knee would bend – those in heavenly realms, on earth and under the earth; and every tongue acknowledge that Jesus Christ is Lord to the glory of God the father.

Therefore, my beloved friends, as you have always been obedient, not only when I was with you but even more when I am not, so do continue to work out your salvation with fear and trembling. And God is working within you, inspiring in you the desire to act to win his approval. Do everything without complaints and arguments so that you may be blameless and innocent – God's children without fault – in the midst of a crooked and perverse generation amongst whom you shine as luminaries in the world, holding up a life-giving message, so that I may boast on the day of Christ, that I did not run **in a useless race** or work in vain. Indeed, even if I am being poured out as a libation to achieve the sacrificial offering of your faith,[1] I am glad and rejoice with all of you, as you should be glad and rejoice with me.

I hope in the Lord Jesus soon to send Timothy to you so that I can be cheered up when I hear news of you. For I have no one comparable to him in his genuine concern for your well being. They are all looking out for their own interest and not those of Jesus Christ. But you appreciate Timothy's character, because in the spreading of the good news he has worked with me as a child under his father. He is the one I hope to send as soon as I see how things are going with me. But I also trust in the Lord that I might also visit you soon.

I also feel compelled to send back to you Epaphroditus, my brother, fellow-worker and fellow-soldier, who was the messenger you sent to minister to my needs. He longs for you all and was troubled over your hearing of his illness. Indeed he was very poorly, even close to death. But God had mercy on him, and not only on him but also on me, to spare me one grief on another. I am, therefore, all the more eager to send him to you, so that seeing him

---

[1] Paul rejoices in imitating Christ by sacrificing himself for the believers.

again, you may rejoice and that will alleviate my own distress. Welcome him in the Lord with great joy and hold those like him in great honour because it was on account of his work for Christ he came close to death, having risked his life to render me those services that you were not able to give me. Finally, brother, rejoice in the Lord.

To repeat what I have already written is no problem for me particularly if it reinforces your resolve. Beware of the dogs, those workers in wickedness, of those who insist on mutilation. For we are the "circumcised" because we worship by the divine spirit and boast only in Jesus Christ and find no **spiritual** security in **the circumcision of** the flesh. If other men think that they can find **spiritual** security in **the circumcision of** the flesh, I can be more secure: of the nation of Israel, of the tribe of Benjamin, Hebrew of Hebrew parents, circumcised on the eighth day, interpreting the Torah – a Pharisee; in terms of religious enthusiasm – a persecutor of the holy community; as for righteousness through the observance of the Torah – faultless!

"For his sake I lost everything"

But whatever spiritual profit I gained from all this I consider a loss in the perspective of Christ. Even more, I consider everything a loss in perspective of the supreme value of knowing my Lord, Jesus Christ. For his sake I lost everything but considered it as refuse so that I might gain Christ and be found in him – not with any righteousness of my own based on the observance of the Torah, but that which is through faith in Christ. This is the righteousness that comes **as a gift** from God earned by faith – to know him, the power of his resurrection and the fellowship of sharing in his sufferings, even being like him in his death, so that somehow I might attain the resurrection of the dead. Not that I believe that I have received this **assurance** or that I have become perfect but I believe that I may take hold of it as Jesus Christ has taken hold of me.

Brothers, I do not think that I have taken hold of it – **the promise of resurrection** – but one thing I do **towards reaching that goal:** the forgetting that which is in the past and pushing forward towards what is ahead. I press forward towards the finishing line to win the prize for which God calls me upward through Jesus Christ. Therefore, let all those who strive for perfection take a similar view. If you should ever think differently, **you will see that** God will reveal its truth to you. Be that as it may, let us not go backward from the place to which we have gone, **that is the acceptance that salvation comes through the cross and not circumcision and the observance of the Torah.**

Brothers, follow my example and take note of those who have lived according to the model I have given you. As I have told you before and tell you now in tears, there are many who live as enemies of the cross of Christ – whose end is destruction. Their stomach is their god and they glory in shamelessness, for they only think about material things. We, however, are citizens of heaven and from there we await the Lord Jesus Christ, our saviour. He will transform our shameful bodies to be like a form of his own glorious body – this by the power which puts everything under his control.

So now, my brothers, as I love and long for you who are my crown and joy, so stand upright in the Lord, my dearly beloved. I implore you, Euodia; I implore you, Syntyche – be reconciled for the **sake of the** Lord. Yes, and I ask you, faithful Syzgus, to help them, who fought together with me – along with Clement and my fellow-workers, whose names are in the book of life – to spread the good news. Always rejoice in the Lord. I say it again: rejoice! Let your gentleness be seen by all men. The Lord is near. Be anxious over nothing, but through prayer and petition and with thanks-giving make your requests on all matters before God. The peace of God which surpasses all understanding will guard your hearts and your thoughts through Jesus Christ.

Finally, brothers, think only about that which is true, that which is honourable, that which is just, that which is pure, that which is worthy of love, that which is admirable – everything of virtue and praiseworthy. Also, practise what you have learned, received, heard or see me do. So will the God of peace be with you.

I greatly rejoice in the Lord that at last you have renewed your concern for me.

I now know that you have been worried **about me** but did not have the opportunity for indicating it. I do not say this because I am in need of anything – I have learnt to cope with whatever conditions I happen to be in. I know both how to live in humble circumstances and in luxury. I have been initiated into the secret of dealing with every situation – satiety and hunger, poverty and plenty. I am capable of everything through he who empowers me.

Still, you do well to share in my affliction. As you know, O Philippians, in the early days of the spreading of the good news, when I left Macedonia, not one of the communities, excepting yourselves, shared in the responsibility of my expenditure and income. Indeed, not once but twice you sent to meet my needs while in Thessalonica. **I am not** saying this because I am looking for presents, but only to credit your account **for your concern and generosity.** I have all I need and more. I am fully provided, especially now that I have received from Epaphroditus your gifts. It is a sweet smelling offering – both acceptable and pleasing to God. And my God will fulfil every need of yours according to his riches in the glory of Jesus Christ.

To our God and father, be glory forever and ever. Amen. Greet every holy one in Jesus Christ. The brothers who are with me greet you. All the holy ones send you greetings, especially those who belong to the Imperial household. The grace of the Lord Jesus Christ be with your spirit. Amen.

Letter to the Colossians

FROM: *Paul an apostle of Jesus Christ by the will of God and Timothy our brother.*
TO: *The holy and faithful brothers in Christ at Colossae.*

Grace and peace to you from God our father. We always give thanks to God, the father of our Lord Jesus Christ when we pray for you because we have heard of your faith in Jesus Christ and of your love for all the holy ones – both being the consequence of the hope **which you believe is** stored up in heaven for you which you already heard about in the truthful words of the good news which had reached you. It is bearing fruit and growing well all over the world as it has with you from the day on which you heard and fully understood the grace of God in all its truth. This you learned from Epaphras, our beloved fellow-servant, who is a true minister of Christ on our behalf and who has also told us of your love awakened by the divine spirit.

Therefore, we too, since the day we heard of this, we did not stop praying on your behalf – asking that you be filled with the knowledge of his will with perfect wisdom and spiritual understanding so that you might live lives worthy of the Lord and pleasing to him in every way: bearing fruit with every good deed, constantly growing towards the full knowledge of God, empowered by the greatness of his glory to endure all with patience and joy; giving thanks to the father who made you fit to share in the portion of the holy ones in the light of God's **redemptive grace.** He has delivered us out of the dominion of darkness and brought us to the Kingdom of his beloved son, in whom we are redeemed and obtain forgiveness from our sins.

He is an image of the invisible God, the firstborn of all creation, because by him were all things in heaven and earth, the visible and invisible, whether thrones, dominions, rulers or authorities – all things through him and for him were created. He is before all things and through him all things are held together.[1] He is the head of the body – the holy community. He is the beginning – the firstborn from the dead[2] so that in all things he has first place. For God was delighted that all his fullness should dwell in him; and that through him all things would be reconciled to himself – making peace both in heaven and on earth through his blood on the cross.

Before that time, you were alienated **from Christ** and mentally hostile **towards him** because of your bad behaviour. Now, he has reconciled you through the death of his earthly body to present you as holy, faultless and irreproachable before him – if you indeed persevere in faith firmly grounded, secure and without shifting from the hope of the good news which you heard proclaimed to all creation under the heavens, of which I, Paul, became a minister.

"I rejoice in my sufferings for your sake"

Now, I rejoice in my sufferings for your sake and I fill up in my flesh the afflictions of Christ which he still has to endure for the sake of his body – his holy community – of which I have become the minister by the commission given me by God to fulfil for you the word of God – the mystery that has been hidden away over the ages and from all generations; but which has now been made known to his holy ones.[3] God desired to make known to them among the nations the riches of the glory of this mystery which is that Christ is in you – the hope of glory **of things to come.** He is whom we proclaim, warning and teaching everyone with all wisdom so that we may perfect everyone in Christ. I labour for this striving with all the power through which he works in me.

I want you to know how hard I am struggling **on your behalf**

---

[1] Rabbinic literature assigns this role to the Torah, which was perceived to be the blueprint for the world's creation.

[2] The first to enjoy resurrection.

[3] Paul here seems to make a claim of pre-eminence over all the other apostles by the nature of his mission to tell of the mystery of Jesus" death on the cross and to share in Christ's suffering.

and for you and for all those in Laodicea and for all those who have never set eyes on me, that their hearts be given courage, that they join together in love, that they may enjoy all the benefits of a complete understanding and knowledge of the mystery of God, both of the father and of Christ in which are hidden all the treasures of wisdom and knowledge. I say this to you so that no one should deceive you with specious argument. Though I am absent from you in body, I am still with you in spirit, and rejoice in your solidarity and firm faith in Christ.

So then as you accepted Jesus Christ as Lord – live in him. Be rooted in him and built up through him, strengthened by the faith you were taught and overflowing with thankfulness **for the gift of grace.** Beware of anyone who through philosophic reasoning and vain speculation based on traditional and worldly prejudices seeks to rob you from Christ. In him is the fullness of the godhead in bodily form, and you are fulfilled in him who is supreme over every power and authority. Through him you were circumcised with a circumcision not performed by human hands but the circumcision of Christ by which you were stripped of your material existence. By your baptism **in Christ** you were buried with him and through faith in God's power you were raised with him from the dead.

When you had died to your sinful nature, though uncircumcised in the flesh, God raised you to life with him, **Christ,** forgiving all our trespasses, erasing the record and laws which were confronting us. He took it away and nailed it to the cross. He stripped away the authority of the rulers; he publicly exposed them and triumphed over them through it – his death on the cross.[1]

Therefore let no person judge you by what you eat or drink, whether in regard to the celebration of a festival, the New Moon or the Sabbaths which are a mere shadow of the things to come. The reality is Christ! Do not be condemned by one who, with seeming humility and respect for the agents of God, claims to have seen things and vainly boast of his human insights into **the divine,** but

---

[1] The humiliation of Christ is in reality his triumph. He is saved while eternal death is their fate.

is not aware of the "head" from which the body through its joints and ligaments and sinews is joined together and grows together according to God's design.

If you died with Christ to the natural world, why should you be subject – as if you were living in this world – to its rules?[1] "Do not touch, nor taste, nor hold." Because they are teachings and laws based on human mores, they will perish. Such rules have the appearance of being wise by its recommendation of self-imposed piety, self-abasement and self-discipline but they do not succeed in restraining the sensuality of the flesh.

As you were raised with Christ, cast your thoughts above where Christ is sitting at the right hand of God. Set your minds on that which is above and not on earthly things, for you have died **to the earth**, and your life lies hidden with Christ in God. Whenever Christ, who is your life, is revealed, you will appear **with him** in glory. Put to death, therefore, the inclinations of your earthly nature: fornication, impurity, passion, lust and the rapacious yearning **for other people's goods** which is as wicked as idolatry, for which things the wrath of God is coming. This was how you behaved when you lived this kind of life. But now, you must rid yourself of all such vices: rage, anger, malice, slander and abusive talk. Do not lie to each other since you have stripped off your old self with its practices and have become a new man – reborn in knowledge in the image of his creator. Here there is no distinction between Hellenist and Jew, circumcised and uncircumcised, barbarian and Scythian, slave and freeman, but Christ is in all and all are in Christ.

Therefore, as the chosen ones of God, holy and beloved, clothe yourselves in deep compassion, kindness, humility, gentleness and patience, bearing with one another and forgiving if you have a grievance against anyone. As the Lord has forgiven you – so must you be forgiven. But supreme over all is love which is the bond of perfection. Let the reconciliation in Christ rule your hearts, since

[1] The Torah is identified with Jesus. When he died, the Torah died with him, as did the curse that was the consequence of not observing the Torah (See p 56, Letters to the Galatians.)

you were called into one body – **Christ,** so be thankful. Let the message of Christ enrich your inner self so that with wisdom you teach and give counsel as you sing psalms, hymns and songs of the spirit with grateful hearts to God. Whatever you do, in speech or in deed, do in the name of the Lord Jesus, giving thanks to God the father through him.

Wives, be subject to your husbands as is proper according to the Lord; husbands, love your wives and do not embitter them; children, obey your parents in all respects for this pleases the Lord; fathers, do not provoke your children or they will lose confidence. Slaves, in all ways obey your masters and not only in their presence to win approval but with sincere hearts in fear of the Lord. Whatever you do, act with sincerity as you were serving the Lord and not men. **Do this** as you know that you will receive the reward of your inheritance from the Lord. You serve the Lord Christ **in whatever you do towards each other**. Those who do wrong will be punished for their wrongdoing. There will be no respect for persons, **husband or wife, parent or child, slave or master in the day of judgement.**

Masters, act with justice and fairness to your slaves in the knowledge that you also have a master in heaven. Persevere in prayers, attentive and with thanksgiving. Pray also for us so that God may open doors for our message – to speak of the mystery of Christ to which I have been bound that I may reveal it as forcefully as I should. Be sensitive in your behaviour towards outsiders but make the most of every opportunity **to bring them to Christ**. Let your words be gracious, seasoned with salt so that your answers to everyone are tasteful.

Tychicus will give you all the news about me. He is a beloved brother and loyal minister and fellow-servant in the Lord. I send him to you for this very purpose in order that you might hear about our situation and that he might lift your morale; he comes with Onesimus, our loyal and beloved brother who is one of you. They will inform you about all things happening here. Aristarchus, my fellow prisoner, and Mark, Barnabas's cousin (you have already received my instructions about him – if he comes to you – welcome him). Jesus, the one called Justus, who is among the few of my fellow workers for the kingdom of God who are circumcised and who give me support, also sends greetings to you.

Epaphras, one of you, a servant of Jesus Christ, is always in prayer, wrestling on your behalf that you stand firm, convinced and committed totally to the will of God. I am his witness that he is deeply concerned for you and those in Laodicea and Hierapolis – he too greets you. The beloved Luke – the physician – and Demas send greetings. Give my greetings to the brothers in Laodicea and to Nympha, and the holy community who meet in her home. Once this letter is read to you, let it be read to the holy community of Laodicians. You in return should read the letter sent to the Laodicians.[1] And tell Archippus: "See to it that you fulfil the ministry which you have received from the Lord.

I, Paul, write this greeting in my own hand. Remember that I am in chains. Grace be with you.

[1] This could be the letter to the Ephesians

Letter to the Ephesians[1]

FROM: *Paul, an apostle of Jesus Christ by the will of God.*
TO: *The holy ones in Ephesus, the faithful in Jesus Christ.*

Grace and peace to you from God our father and the Lord Jesus Christ. Praised be the God and the father of our Lord Jesus Christ, he who has blessed us with every spiritual blessing in Christ in the realms of heaven. Before the foundations of the earth were established he chose us through Christ to become holy and faultless in love before him, and he predestined us to become his adopted sons through Jesus Christ. This was his purpose and pleasure to win praise for the glory of his gracious gift to us through the one he loved. In him, through his blood, we are redeemed, we are forgiven our sins in accordance with the riches of his gifts which he lavished on us all wisdom and understanding. He made known to us the mystery of his purpose in Christ to be fulfilled when the time was ripe – to unite all things in heaven and earth under one head – Christ.

In him we were also chosen, predestined by the purpose of God who creates everything in accordance to his will – that we who were the first to place our hope in Christ should cause his glory to be praised.[2] You also are in Christ, once you heard the true word, the good news of your salvation and believed – in him you have been stamped with the seal of the promise of the holy spirit which is the first portion of our **divine** inheritance until the final redemption of those who belong to God – for the praise of his glory.

Therefore, since I heard about your faith in the Lord Jesus and

[1] There is some doubt whether this letter was dictated by Paul. As it reflects Paul's theology, particularly his interest in Christ the resurrected over the Jesus who lived in the flesh, I am happy to include it among his writings, even if it was written by one of his disciples.
[2] From what follows is it possible that Paul is referring to himself as being the first to place his hope in Christianity, i.e. the other apostles knew Jesus in the flesh, he knew him as the Son-of-God? In his letters he often uses the first person plural – the majestic we!

your love for all the holy ones **in his communities**, I have not stopped giving thanks for you, making mention of you always in my prayers, so that the God of our Lord Jesus Christ, the father of glory, may give you the spirit of wisdom and revelation to know him more fully; also that the eyes of your heart be enlightened for you to realise the hope his call holds out to you and how great is the glory of his inheritance for his holy ones; and how great **the sources of** his power to us who believe in him. It is the great exercise of power which he used in raising Christ from the dead and placing him on his right hand in the realms of heaven, above all governments and authorities, powers and lords and any title that commands subservience, now in this age and in all the ages to come. God subjected everything under his feet, to be the head of everyone in the community **of believers**, which is his body in which is the fullness of the God of all things who fills everything.

And you were **spiritually** dead because of your trespasses and sins when you followed the ways of the contemporary world in obedience to the "Sovereign of Superficiality'[1] – **Satan –** whose influence works in the sons of rebellion – among whom we were numbered when we lived according to the desires of our flesh, succumbing to its demands and its perspectives **of life.** Like the rest of them, by our very nature we were liable to **God's** anger **and condemnation.** But God, rich in compassion because of the greatness of the love with which he loved us, even though we were **spiritually** dead through our trespasses, brought us into life through Christ.[2] **Only** by **divine** grace have you been saved.

God has raised us and seated us in the realms of heaven through Jesus Christ so that in the age to come he might reveal the supreme riches of his gracious kindness towards us through Jesus Christ. Through faith you have been saved by his grace. This is not of your own doing – it is the gift of God. It is not due to **good** works so that

---

[1] My paraphrase of the Greek. Literally "the ruler of the authority over the air".
[2] The Pharisaic Jewish view was that the Torah was the Tree of Life and that, even if one broke its rules, God would in his compassion forgive the repentant sinner, namely he who is filled with remorse for his action and does not commit the same sin in similar circumstances.

no one should boast **of his righteousness.** We are God's creation in Jesus Christ to do good works which God had made ready for us to practice.

"They were reconciled to God through the cross"

Therefore, remember that when you by birth were Gentiles, referred to as the uncircumcised by those who are called "the circumcised" – a physical operation formed by the hand **of man**; remember that you were then without Christ – alienated from the commonwealth of Israel and strangers to her covenants of the **divine** promise, hopeless and godless in your world! But now, you through Jesus Christ, you who were far off, have come near through the blood of Christ. He himself is the source of our harmony. He made us both – **Jews by birth and Gentiles in Christ** – a unity; the dividing wall of hostility **between the two** he has broken down – through **the sacrifice of** his flesh, he abolished the Torah of commandments with its edicts. This he did that he might create out of the two – **Gentile and Jew** – one new man and so make reconciliation. Through both being in one body – **Christ** – they were reconciled to God through the cross because **as both Jew and Gentile believed that he died for them, that they were both in his body,** God destroyed the hostility **between them** through him.[1]

He, **Jesus**, came and preached peace both to those who were far off and to those who were near and, because of this, through him we both have access to the father through one **divine** spirit. Consequently you are no longer either strangers or aliens, but are fellow citizens of the holy ones and members of God's family,[2] built on the foundations of the apostles and prophets with Jesus Christ being himself its cornerstone – in him the whole building holds together and becomes a holy temple in the Lord. Also, in him, you are together built up to become a spiritual dwelling for God.

---

[1] I would think that it is to Jesus that the verse refers and not to God.
[2] He is referring to the Jews. Christ becomes the replacement of the temple as God's home.

For this reason, I, Paul, have become a prisoner of Jesus Christ for the sake of you Gentiles. Indeed, you must have heard that I was given the responsibility for dispensing the grace of God given to me to give to you. Through revelation, the mystery **of Christ** was made known to me. I have already briefly written about this. By reading this you can learn of my understanding of the mystery of Christ which has not been made known in the past generations to the sons of men but which now has been revealed by the spirit to his holy apostles and prophets – the Gentiles have become co-heirs, members of the same body **with Israel** and co-sharers in the promise of Jesus Christ through the good news of which I became a minister by the gift of God's grace given to me through the workings of his power.

To me, the least of all the holy ones, this grace was given to proclaim the unfathomable riches of Christ to the Gentiles and bring to light the meaning of that mystery which throughout the ages has been hidden by God the creator of all things. **This he did** so that now through the **holy** community **of Christ** the multi-faceted wisdom of God should be made known to the rulers and authorities in the realms of heaven. This is consistent with an age-old purpose to be accomplished in Jesus Christ our Lord and through whom, because of our faith in him, *we* approach God with pride and confidence.

I ask you, therefore, not to be disheartened by my sufferings on your behalf. This is to your honour. For this reason I bend my knees to the father from whom every family in heaven and earth derives its nature that, through the magnificence of his glory, he strengthens you by the power of his spirit in your inner being – that Christ through the faith of your hearts may live in you; and that you, rooted and grounded in love, will have the power together with all the holy ones to understand how broad, how long, how high and how deep – knowing that this love of Christ surpasses knowledge, you will overflow with the fullness of God.

To him who through his power working within us is able to accomplish more than we could ever desire or imagine; to him be glory in the holy community and in Jesus Christ from generation to generation and from age to age. Amen.

As a prisoner of the Lord, I implore you to live a life worthy of the calling you received, with all humility and gentleness, with patience, supporting each other in love, always eager to be united in the spirit through the bond of reconciliation. There is one body and one spirit – as in your calling, you were called in one hope, one Lord, one faith, one baptism, one God and father of all, through all and in all.[1] Yet to each one of us was given grace in accordance to the allocation of Christ's gift. This is why it says, "When he ascended on high he took captives and gave gifts to men" [Psalm 68:18]. Now what does "he ascended" imply except that he also descended to the lower regions of the earth? He who descended is also the one who ascended far above all the heavens in order to fill all things. **What were his gifts?** His gifts were that some should be apostles, some prophets, some the messengers of the good news, some pastors and teachers – to enable the holy ones, **the believers,** to perform the tasks of his ministry by building up the body – **the holy community** – of Christ until all of us arrive at a unity of faith and of the full knowledge of the Son-of-God, each becoming a perfect person by attaining the full stature of Christ.

No more will we be **vulnerable** infants, blown and carried off here and there by every new wind of erroneous teaching from men agile in shrewdness and deceit. Rather, will we speak truthfully in love, we will grow up into him in all ways. He is the head, that is Christ, whose whole body is fitted and joined together by every supporting ligament, making the body grow by each part building it up in love. **The body is the holy community and each of us, apostles, prophets, bearers of good tidings, pastors and teachers, are the parts which make the body strong according to the gifts we have received.**

Therefore I say this to you and give witness in **the name of** the

[1] Normally, the mystical experience is deeply personal – the loss of individuality. What Paul is describing is a mystical existence for an entire group. Unity of faith in Christ enables all the believers as one entity to become part of the godhead.

Lord: "Live no more as do the Gentiles guided by their air-headed brains." Their intellects have been clouded over so that they are alienated from the godly life because of their ignorance which is due to their stubborn wilfulness. Because of their callousness, they have surrendered themselves to licentiousness and indulge in every perversion. That is not what you have learnt from Christ, if indeed you heard of him and were taught the truth of Jesus: that you put away your former way of life, your old selves corrupted by misleading lustfulness, and be reborn with a new spirit and attitude of mind – to become new men created according to the likeness of God in righteousness and the holiness of truth.

Therefore you must divest yourself of falsehood and each person speaking truthfully to his neighbour because we are each members of one body. When you are angry do not sin and do not let the sun set while you are still nursing your anger lest you give the devil a foothold. The one who steals **for a living** must steal no more but do honest labour with his own hands that he may have something to contribute to those in need. Do not be crude in your speech but speak positively to bolster up those who are listening according to their needs. Do not give grief to the divine spirit of God who has put his seal upon you for the day of redemption. Let all bitterness, rage, anger, loudness and slander part from you together with all that is wicked. Act towards each other with kindness and softness of heart, forgiving each other, just as God through Christ has forgiven you.

Be imitators of God. As beloved children, live a life of love as Christ loved you and gave himself up for us as a sweet smelling offering and sacrifice to God. Let there be no trace of licentiousness, impurity or lust as this would be improper for holy people. Rather than vulgarity, foolish talk and joking which is unbecoming, let there be thanksgiving **to God!** Know for certain that every lecher, immoral or avaricious person, being the equivalent of an idolater – will have no inheritance in the Kingdom of Christ and God. Let no one deceive you with empty words because through them descends the wrath of God on those who are rebellious. Therefore be not their partners.

Once you lived in darkness, but now you live in the light of the Lord. Live as children of light, for the fruit of light is all goodness, righteousness and truth. Seek to do what pleases the Lord and have nothing to do with the unfruitful works of darkness, but rather expose them **for what they are.** It is embarrassing even to speak of what they do under the cover of secrecy. But everything is revealed under the glare of light, for light is what makes everything visible. Therefore it is said, "Rise, O sleeping ones, rise up from the dead and Christ will shine on you."

Be careful, therefore, in the way you live – not foolishly but wisely, using the time to advantage because we are living in evil times. Do not be foolish and be aware of the will of the Lord. Do not get drunk with wine for this leads to debauchery, but be intoxicated with the divine spirit: recite psalms, hymns and spiritual songs amongst yourselves. Sing and use your hearts as harps of the Lord, always strumming thanks for everything to God the father in the name of our Lord Jesus Christ. Be subject to each other out of reverence for Christ – the wives to their husbands as to the Lord because the man is the head of a woman as Christ is the head of the holy community – his body of which he is the saviour. And as the community is subject to Christ so are wives in everything subject to their husbands.

"He who loves his wife loves himself"

Husbands! Love your wives **just** as Christ loves the holy community and surrendered himself for her sake to make her holy by washing her with cleansing water through his words in order to present her to himself in splendour without a spot or wrinkle or any such disfigurement so that she might be divine and without blemish. So too should husbands love their wives as they do their own bodies. He who loves his wife loves himself, for no man hates his own body but feeds it and cares for it, just as Christ does the holy community, because we are part of his body. "For this reason a man shall leave his father and his mother and clings to his wife and the two of them become one flesh" [Genesis 2:24]. This is a profound mystery as **to what I am saying about** Christ's relationship to the holy community. **But in every other respect,** let each one of you love his wife as he loves himself in order that she reveres her husband.

Children, obey your parents for it is right to do so. "Honour your father and your mother," which is the very first commandment to be coupled with a **reward:** "So that it may be well with you and that you may enjoy a long life on the earth" [Deuteronomy 5:16]. Fathers, do not make your children angry with resentment against your authority, but raise them well disciplined in the teaching of the Lord. Slaves, obey your earthly lords with fear and trembling and a sincerity of heart just as you do Christ, not just when he sees you and in order to please him, but like slaves of Christ, doing God's will out of the depths of one's soul with good will as you were serving the Lord and not humans. Do this in the knowledge that the Lord will reciprocate whatever good a man does whether he is a slave or a freeman. Masters, act in the same manner towards them, patient but not threatening with the realisation that he who is master of you both is in heaven and that he is no respecter of persons **when he sits in judgement.**

Finally, draw your strength from the Lord and his enabling power. Dress yourself in the full armour of God so that you are able to withstand the deviousness of the devil, for our struggle is not with flesh and blood, but against the rulers, authorities and sovereigns of this world of darkness; also against spiritual powers of evil in the realms of heaven. Wherefore, dress in the full armour of God to enable you to resist them on the evil day and, having done everything possible, to stand firm. Stand, therefore, your waist girded with truth and your chest with the breastplate of righteousness and your feet shod with readiness to proclaim the good news of peace. At all times, wear the shield of faith with which you can put out the flaming arrows of the evil one. Take the helmet of salvation and the sword of the spirit which is the word of God. At every opportunity, with all kinds of prayer and petition, pray in the spirit. To that end, keep watch and persevere in praying for all the holy ones.

Pray also for me that, when I open my mouth, the words be given to me to courageously make known the mystery of the good news for whom I am an ambassador in chains, so that I have the courage to speak as is my duty.

Tychicus, the beloved brother and faithful servant of the Lord, will tell you everything about me and what I have been doing. I am sending him to you for this very purpose so that you may know all about us and so that he may refresh your hearts with encouragement. Peace to the brothers and love with faith from God the father and the Lord Jesus Christ. Grace to all those who love our Lord Jesus Christ with an undying love.

Letter to Philemon

FROM: *Paul, a prisoner of Jesus Christ and Timothy our brother.*
TO: *Philemon, our beloved friend and fellow worker;*
Apphia, our sister;
Archippus, our fellow soldier and
The holy community which assembles at your home.

Grace to you and peace from God our father and the Lord Jesus Christ. I always thank my God as I remember you in my prayers because I hear of the love and faith you have in the Lord Jesus and **your love** for all the holy ones. May the fellowship of faith create in you a full appreciation of all the goodness we have through Christ. Great is my joy and comfort over your love because through you, brother, the hearts of the holy ones are lifted up. Though in Christ, I could be demanding in instructing as to what you must do, rather would I plead with you on the basis of love.

I speak to you then, **not as an apostle, but only** as Paul, an old man, and now also a prisoner of Jesus Christ. I appeal to you for Onesimus[1] who while I was in chains acted as my adopted child. Formerly, he was of no use to you. Now, however, he has become useful both to you and me. I send him back to you – he who is to me as my own heart. I resolved to keep him here so that he could minister to me on your behalf while I am imprisoned because of the good news **I am bringing.** But, without your counsel, I would do nothing, so that whatever goodness you do for me you do voluntarily and not under duress.

Might it not be that he left you for a little time, so that you could now have him back for good, but no longer as a slave, but even more beneficial than a slave – a beloved brother **in Christ**, especially to me, and even much more to you both as a person and **a brother** in the Lord. So, if you consider me as a partner, welcome

---

[1] The literal meaning of the name is "useful" which is the basis of Paul's playful description.

him as you would me. If he has wronged you or owes you anything, charge my account.[1] **I am utterly sincere in this matter.** Therefore I write with my own hand that I will pay it back, **in spite of the fact that** I could say that you are in debt to me for your whole life, **as I have saved you through Christ.**

Brother, I do hope that I may have some help from you because of the Lord. **By your response,** recreate my heart in Christ. Trusting in your compliance **to my appeal,** I wrote to you in the knowledge that you will do even more than I ask. Also, prepare for me some lodging, for I hope that through your prayers **on my behalf** I shall be granted leave to visit you.

Epaphrus, my fellow-prisoner in Jesus Christ, sends greetings, as do Mark, Aristarchus, Demas and Luke, my fellow workers. The grace of the Lord Jesus Christ be with your spirit.

[1] Onesimus must have been Philemon's slave who left him under pressure from Paul, whose future Paul now wants to secure.

Appendix

CHAPTER 16:5-16

Greet also the holy community that meets at their [Priscilla's and Aquila's] home. Greet my beloved friend, Epaenetus, who was the first fruit [convert] to Christ in Asia. Greet Mary who has done many things for you. Greet Andronicus and Junius, my kinsmen, who were in prison with me. They were notable among the apostles.[1] Indeed, they were in Christ before I was. Greet Ampliatus, who is my beloved companion in the Lord. Greet Urbanus, our fellow-worker in Christ, and Stachys, my beloved friend. Greet Apelles who has been found worthy of Christ. Greet the household of Aristobulus. Greet Herodion, my kinsman.[2] Greet the household of Narcissus who are in the Lord. Greet Tryphaena and Tryphosa who labour for the Lord. Greet the beloved Persis who does many things for the Lord. Greet Rufus, chosen by the Lord, and his mother who has been as a mother to me. Greet Asyncritus, Phlegon, Hermes, Patrobas, Hermas and the brothers who are with him. Greet Philoloqus and Julia, Nereus, his sister, and Olympas and all the holy ones who are with them. Greet one another with a holy kiss. To all the holy communities of Christ give greetings.

CHAPTER 16:21-24

Timothy, my fellow-worker, sends greetings to you as do Lucius, Jason and Sosipater, my kinsmen. I, Tertius, who was the scribe for this letter, greet you in the Lord. Gaius, my host, and of the entire holy community, greets you, as do Erastus, the town's treasurer, and his brother Quartus.

---

[1] They are not mentioned as being among the apostles and their home was in Rome. For this reason, commentators have interpreted this to mean that the apostles had taken notice of them. It is more likely that the word "apostle" meaning "messenger" or "one sent" was a more encompassing term than it came to be. Paul himself was never elected as an apostle in the strictest sense of the word, as was Matthias to replace Judas as the Twelfth [Acts 1:23-26].
[2] This is the third kinsman he refers to. While some translations interpret this to mean "relative", I would think that he is referring to compatriots, meaning either Jews or individuals from his own town, Tarsus, or from his province Glicia.

APPENDIX 2 · SECOND LETTER TO THE THESSALONIANS

FROM: *Paul, Silvanus and Timothy.*
TO: *The holy community of Thessalonians who are in God our father and the Lord Jesus Christ.*

Grace and peace be to you from God the father and the Lord Jesus Christ. We must always give thanks to God regarding you, brothers, and rightly so because your faith grows stronger and your love for one another continues to increase. We ourselves boast over you throughout the holy communities of God because of your perseverance and faith in spite of all the persecutions and distress you are enduring – a certain token of the justice of God's judgement for this will be added to your account of worthiness to enter God's Kingdom for which you indeed suffer.

It will be justice for God to repay with affliction those who afflicted you, and to give rest to you and to us when the Lord Jesus is revealed from heaven with his mighty messengers in flames of fire, rendering judgement against those who did not acknowledge God and to those who did not heed the good news of our Lord Jesus. They will pay the penalty of eternal destruction, cut off from the face of the Lord and from the glory of his might, whenever he comes to be glorified in his holy people and to be adored by all those who believed in him – including yourselves who believed in the testimony we gave you.

That is why we always pray concerning you so that our God may deem you worthy of his calling and through his power fulfil each good purpose and every act of faith; so may the name of our Lord Jesus be glorified through you and you in him according to the grace of our God and Lord Jesus Christ.

Now, as to the coming of our Lord Jesus Christ and our being gathered to him, we ask you, brothers, not to let your minds be unsettled nor alarmed not by a "spirit" nor through words or a letter attributed to us saying that the day of the Lord has come. Let no one deceive you in any of these ways. That day cannot come before the **final** rebellion and the man of wickedness is revealed:

the son of perdition – the one who opposes and exalts himself over every so-called God or is an object of worship, even to himself seating himself in God's temple proclaiming himself to be god.[1]

Do you not remember me telling you this when I was with you? Now you know what is restraining him – and the time when he will be revealed. The mystery of wickedness is now at work, but let him who is holding it back be removed, and the wicked one will be revealed whom the Lord Jesus will destroy by a breath of his mouth and will reduce to nothingness by the radiant appearance of his coming. The coming **of the wicked one** will be made apparent in the working of Satan with every great power and miracles and wonders that deceive, with all the deceptions of the wicked, those who will perish because they rejected the love of truth which would have saved them. Therefore, God sends them an illusory power which makes them believe in a lie so that all who did not believe in the truth but took pleasure in wickedness might be condemned.[2]

But we must always thank God for you, brothers, loved by the Lord, because God chose you to be the first fruits of his salvation by the sanctification of the divine spirit and the faith in truth; to which he called you through our good news that you might share in the glory of our Lord Jesus Christ. So, brothers, stand firm and hold fast to the teachings you were taught by us in person or through our letters. May our Lord Jesus Christ himself and God our father, who loved us and through whose grace we have been given eternal comfort and enormous hope, may he give comfort to your hearts and may he fortify you in every good word and deed.

Finally, pray for us, brothers, so that the message of the Lord may spread quickly and be glorified as it was with you; and that we

[1] One would not expect this fixed view of the timing of Jesus" coming from Paul. In Thessalonians I, he writes that "you all know that it will come suddenly as a thief in the night." Paul did not believe that the imminent coming of Christ was dependent on a final battle between "Satan" and God.

[2] According to this teaching there is no middle ground. Those who did not accept the love of Christ would be ensnared into the camp of Satan in order that they might become wicked and justifiably condemned. This too does not reflect Paul's attitude.

may be spared from corrupt and evil men, for not all men are faithful. But the Lord is faithful. He will strengthen you and protect you from evil. We have confidence in the Lord that you are acting and will act according to our instructions. May the Lord direct your hearts into the love of God and the patience of Christ.

Now, we charge you, brothers, in the name of the Lord Jesus Christ to avoid every brother who lives an idle life and not by the teachings which you received from us. You yourselves know how you should emulate us. We were not idle when we were with you. We accepted no presents of food from anyone. Rather we struggled and worked day and night – labouring so as not to burden any of you **with our up-keep**. Not that our authority did not entitle us to this but in order to set an example for you to follow. When we were with you, we taught you this: He who does not wish to work, let him not eat! We have heard that some among you walk around in idleness, doing no work but meddling in the work of others. We charge and admonish such people in the Lord Jesus Christ to work without making a fuss in order to deserve the food they eat.

And you, brothers, do not be discouraged from doing good. If anyone does not heed the words we send you in this letter, point out this man and do not fraternise with him so that he may be embarrassed; but do not regard him as an enemy but admonish him as a brother. May the Lord of peace himself give you peace always and in every way. The Lord be with you all.

This greeting written in my hand – Paul's – which is the sign of every letter I write.[1] The grace of our Lord Jesus Christ be with all of you.

---

[1] I consider this over-the-top affirmation as further evidence that this letter was not, in fact, written by Paul.

APPENDIX 3 · FIRST LETTER TO TIMOTHY

FROM: *Paul, an apostle of Jesus Christ, by the order of God our saviour and Jesus Christ, our hope.*
TO: *Timothy, a true child of the faith.*
Grace, mercy and peace from God the father and Jesus Christ our Lord.

As I requested that you remain in Ephesus – when I left for Macedonia – to direct certain individuals not to teach dissentient views nor to give any need to false myths and endless genealogical tables **to prove their arguments.** These stir up doubts rather than making them stewards of God through the **foundations** of faith.

The ultimate objective of this instruction is love, coming out of a pure heart, a good conscience and a sincere faith. Some have strayed from these **goals** to talk nonsense. They want to be teachers of the law, but they do not even understand what they themselves are saying no less than that which they assert with such utter confidence. Now, we know that the Torah can be effective if used properly. But we also know that laws are not devised for righteous people but for lawbreakers, the unruly, the godless, sinners, scoffers and the irreligious.

Laws are needed for patricides, matricides,[1] murderers, the promiscuous,[2] pederasts, kidnappers, liars, perjurers and any other activity that is in opposition to the sensible teaching of the good news of the glorious and blessed God with which I was entrusted. I am thankful to our Lord Jesus Christ who, because he found me trustworthy, empowered me, he appointed me into his ministry. **This he did in spite of the fact that** I had formerly been a blasphemer and a contemptuous persecutor of the believers. I found mercy because I acted in my ignorance and lack of faith. Our Lord favoured me with a superabundance of grace accompanied by the faith and love in Jesus Christ.

True is the word that requires universal recognition: "Jesus

[1] The fact that these crimes of killing one's parents are at the top of the list may be an indication that then as now there were more domestic crimes than others.
[2] Literally: fornicators. The intention is the sinfully promiscuous, e.g. adulterers, those engaging in incest, etc.

Christ came into the world to save sinners" – I myself am the greatest of them. For this very reason, I was shown mercy to prove how long suffering was Jesus Christ **in that he forgave me** and as an example for those who by believing in him would be granted eternal life. So, now to the ancient king – immortal and invisible – the only God be honour and glory from everlasting to everlasting. Amen.

Timothy, my child, I commit to you this charge in keeping with the prophecies made about you, to encourage you because of them to fight the good fight with faith and a clear conscience. Some have rejected the **principles** and have shipwrecked their faith. Among these are Hymenaeus and Alexander whom I deliver to Satan to teach them the punishment of blasphemy.

So in your instruction to the Ephesians, I urge you as the first priority that petitions, prayers, intercessions and prayers of thanksgiving be asked for everyone – for kings and all those in authority – that we may live tranquil and quiet lives with piety and decency. This is right and acceptable to God our saviour who wishes all men to be saved and to achieve the complete knowledge of the truth: There is only one God and one mediator between God and man – the man, Jesus Christ, who gave himself as ransom price for all **humanity** – to be proven at its appointed time.

For which purpose I was appointed as herald and apostle. I speak the truth. I do not lie. I am the teacher of faith and truth to the Gentiles. I want men everywhere to lift us their holy hands in prayer without anger and without doubt. Also women should wear appropriate clothes – discreet and modestly, not to adorn themselves with braided hair, with gold or pearls or expensive clothes, but that which is appropriate for women professing to doing good works. During instruction a woman should be silent and reserved. I do not permit women to teach or to exercise authority over men. She must remain in silence. Remember, Adam was created first, then Eve. Also Adam was not seduced **by the serpent** but the woman, being seduced, became a sinner. But she can be saved through childbearing if they persevere in **the virtues of** faith, love, holiness and sensible living.

True is the saying: the person who aspires to be an overseer **of the holy community** desires a noble task. But the overseer must be beyond reproach, a one-wife husband, temperate, sensible, courteous, hospitable and a skilful teacher; not an immoderate drinker, not violent but patient, non-confrontational and not avaricious. He must be able to keep his own household in order, raising his children to obey and respect him. [If a person cannot manage his own household, how can he manage the community of God?] He should not be a recent convert because **due to his hasty promotion** he could become arrogant and come under the same condemnation as the devil. He should have a good reputation with outsiders, so that he does not fall into disrepute **through their standards** and fall into a devil's trap **through the need to defend himself.**

Administrators[1] must also be men of sobriety, not devious **but honest,** not alcoholics, not pursuing dishonest gain but believing in the mystery of the faith with a clear conscience. First let them prove themselves. If they are irreproachable men, let them serve! Women administrators need also be serious in their demeanour, not slanderers but sober and reliable in all things. Administrators should be one-wife husbands able to manage their children and households. Those who serve efficiently will achieve an excellent position for themselves and fortification in their faith in Jesus Christ.

While I hope to come to see you soon, I write these things to you so that if I am delayed you should know how one ought to behave in the household of God which is the community of the living God, the pillar and bulwark of the truth. Without doubt, the mystery of **our** faith is very deep:

He who appeared in the flesh
Was vindicated in the spirit

[1] The Greek is *Daikonous*, meaning servant, translated by me as administrator because it appeared to be the office looking after the secular concerns of the community. This would allow the possibility of women Deacons which would not have been possible had it been a "spiritual" ministry.

Was seen by the Messenger of God
Was proclaimed to the Gentiles,
Was believed in throughout the world and
Was taken up in glory.

Now the Spirit has predicted that in later times there will be some who will leave the faith and go after misleading spirits and demonic teachings – because of men who are hypocritical liars whose consciences have been branded **with a hot iron.** They forbid people to marry and prohibit the eating of foods which God created to be accepted with thanksgiving by those who believe and have full knowledge of the truth. Because all God's creations are good and nothing need be rejected if it is received with thanksgiving – it is made holy by the word of God and the prayer **of thanksgiving.**

If you point this out to the brothers, you will be a good minister of Jesus Christ, being nourished by the words of faith and the good teaching you have followed. But, reject false myths and old wives tales. Train yourself in piety. Of course, physical training is some what beneficial, but **training in** piety is beneficial in every possible way – it holds the promise for both the **physical** life now and the life to come. Truthful is the word that requires universal recognition – for which we work and struggle – that we have set our hope on the living God who is the saviour of all men and especially of believers.

Therefore give these charges and teachings. Do not let anyone despise you because you are so young, but set an example for believers by your speech and practice through love, faith and piety. Until I come, devote yourself to the public reading of the Holy Writings by preaching and teaching them. Do not neglect your gift which was given to you – the prophetic spirit – through the laying of hands on you by the body of elders.[1] Attend to these matters with diligence so that everyone can see your progress.

---

[1] Including Paul. This reminds one of Moses giving of his divine spirit to Joshua through the laying on of hands.

Be conscientious in your practice and teaching. Persevere in this, for in doing so, you will save both yourself and those who listen to you.

Do not rebuke an older man but treat him as you would your father, younger men as brothers, older women as mothers and younger women as sisters; **but do so** with total innocence. Respect **and give financial support** to those in permanent **and single** widowhood. But if a widow has children or grandchildren **who could support them,** let them show their piety by making their first priority the caring of their own family, and so reciprocating the care they received from their parents and grandparents. For this is what pleases God. The forsaken widow, being left on her own, sets her hope on God and is continually making petitions and saying her prayers night and day. But the wanton widow has died **to God** even though she is **very much** alive. So give them these instructions so that they will be free from criticism: if anyone does not provide for his own kinsmen and especially his immediate family, he has denied the faith and is worse than an unbeliever.[1]

No widow should be on the **communal** list **for financial support** unless she is over sixty and has only had one husband and there is evidence of her good works, namely, looking after children, hospitality for strangers, washing the feet of holy men and given help to those afflicted – or the following in the path of doing any good deed. But refuse support to younger widows, for they stray from Christ when they wish to marry. **In desiring** this, they bring retribution on themselves because they have broken their first obligation.[2] Besides, they are inclined to idleness and go from house to house, and worse than idleness, they become gossips and busybodies and speak mischievously.

[1] This stricture certainly suggests in the controversy between "acts and faith" that the author – would it carry more weight if he is Paul? – considers a person who does not behave responsibly as not saved by his faith in Christ.
[2] This stricture is consistent with Paul's call for people not to alter their personal status as they wait for Christ to usher in the Kingdom of God and the final judgement, which he felt would happen in his lifetime.

So I advise younger women[1] to marry, to bear children and to be the mistresses of their homes and so thus not to give unfriendly people the opportunity to reproach them. There have been some who have already left us to follow Satan. Women believers who have widows **in their family** should assist them and not let the holy community be burdened with them. The community should help those "real" widows, **those who are old without the chance of remarrying and who have no families to support them.**

The efficient elders **of the holy community** are due double **financial** consideration, especially those whose efforts are directed towards preaching and teaching. For the writings say, "You shall not muzzle an ox while it is treading out the grain [Deuteronomy 25:4] and the workman works for his wages." [Luke 10:7] Also, do not hear any accusation **of fraud** against an elder unless there are two or three witnesses. But those who are guilty must be reproved publicly so that others may be forewarned.

Before God and Jesus Christ and his chosen divine messengers as my witnesses, I charge you to keep these rules without partiality and do not act instinctively. Do not be quick to lay hold of someone nor be influenced by the wickedness of others, but keep yourself pure and innocent.

You should give up drinking only water. Have some wine for the sake of your digestion to prevent your frequent sicknesses.

Remember also that the sins of some men are quickly apparent before anyone brings them **to the courts** for judgement, but the sins of some are not discovered until much later on. Likewise the good that some people do may be obvious, but even those that are not so apparent will ultimately not be hidden.

All those under the yoke of slavery should consider that their masters are deserving of respect, so that the name of God and our

---

[1] This must refer to widows, but, if so, it is in opposition to the earlier stricture against a change in status which prevents one from focussing on the coming of Christ. It is another of Paul's compromises: i.e. "better to marry than to burn . . ."

teaching are not slandered.[1] And even those whose masters are believers should not show them less respect because they are brothers **in Christ.** On the contrary, they should even render them greater service because they who benefit from it are believers and loved by them. This is what you must teach and encourage them to do.

Anyone who teaches differently **from us** and does not agree with the good sense of the instruction from our Lord Jesus Christ and his true teachings, he is arrogant and without comprehension. He has been infected by futile questions and debates which only lead to envy, strife, blasphemies, baseless suspicions, perpetual wrangling between men of distorted minds who have been deprived of the truth and who think that religion is the means of financial gain. Religion does bring enormous gain but only to those who are satisfied with what they already have. We brought nothing into the world nor can we take anything out. Having food and clothing – we are satisfied. People who are determined to be rich fall into temptation and a trap – the many foolish and dangerous ambitions which cause them to sink into ruin and destruction. For the root of all evil is the love of money – because of which, those who were in pursuit of it strayed from the faith and consequently brought many griefs upon themselves.

But you who are a man of God – flee from such things! Pursue righteousness, piety, faith, love, endurance and humility. Fight the good fight of the faith. Lay hold on eternal life to which you were called and **to** which you responded by confirming your profession in the presence of many witnesses. Before God who gives life to all things and before Jesus Christ, who testified before Pontius Pilate the confession **of truth,** I charge you to keep this commandment with total purity and without cause for reproach until the appearance of our Lord Jesus Christ, whom God will reveal at the time **he**

---

[1] The Christian communities did not wish to be accused of destabilising the social mores. Were slaves who were believers to think themselves superior to their masters of no faith, they would cause disharmony and give Christians a bad name.

wishes – God the blessed one, the only Potentate, the King of kings and the Lord of lords, the only immortal, who lives in impenetrable light whom no man has seen nor ever can see. To him be honour and power forever. Amen.

Charge those who are rich in the present age not to be arrogant nor to set their hope on their uncertain wealth, but only on God who offers us all his riches for our enjoyment – **charge them** to do good, to be rich in good works, ready to give and to be generous – laying up treasures for themselves as a good foundation for the future, so that they may take hold on the life that is real.

O Timothy, guard what has been entrusted to you. Turn away from worldly and empty words which our opponents mistakenly refer to as "knowledge". Some have professed this knowledge as **their faith** and have strayed from the **true** faith. Grace be with you.

APPENDIX 4 · SECOND LETTER TO TIMOTHY

FROM: *Paul, an apostle of Jesus Christ by the will of God according to the promise of life in Jesus Christ.*
TO: *Timothy, my beloved child.*

Grace, mercy, peace from God our father and our Lord Jesus Christ. I give thanks to God whom I worship as did my forefathers with a clear conscience just as night and day I always remember you in my prayers. Having been reminded of your tears, I long to see you to be filled with joy. I am reminded of your unfeigned faith which was first instilled in Lois, your grandmother and then in Eunice, your own mother. I am now persuaded that it also lives in you.

It is for this reason I remind you to fan the flame which is God's gift which is in you because of my laying of hands on you.[1] For God did not give us a cowardly spirit but of power and of love and of self-discipline. Therefore be not ashamed to give testimony about our Lord or about me, his prisoner. But with me, suffer the hardships that come with teaching the good news – trusting in God's power who has saved us and called us to holiness not because of our achievements but because of his own purpose and **the grace he has given us.**

This grace was given to us through Jesus Christ before the beginning of time. It has only now been revealed through the appearance of our saviour Jesus Christ, who has, on the one hand, nullified death and on the other, revealed life and immortality through the good news, for which I was appointed herald, apostle and teacher. And it is for this cause, I suffer these things. But I am not ashamed for I know whom I have believed and I am convinced that he is able to keep guard of **the hope** I have entrusted to him for that day **when our Lord Jesus Christ will return.**[2]

[1] The transmission of the divine spirit through the laying of hands goes back biblically to Moses laying his hands on Joshua to lead Israel to the Promised Land before his own death. As physical life is given by parents to children, the transmission of spiritual power was considered possible between those who enjoyed the grace of God.
[2] A comparatively muted expression of faith for one who has sacrificed all for Christ.

What you have heard from me, keep as a pattern for sensible instruction in the faith and love in Jesus Christ. Guard the good deposit – **the testimony of faith which will bring them and you eternal life.** Guard it with the help of the divine spirit which lives in us. Do you know that everyone in Asia have turned away from me, including Phygelus and Hermogenes. But may the Lord grant mercy to the family of Onesiphorous because he so often refreshed me and was not embarrassed by my chains. Quite the opposite, when he came to Rome he looked for me until he found me. May the Lord grant him the grace to find mercy from him on that day **of judgement.** You remember very well in how many ways he served me in Ephesus.

Be, therefore, my child, empowered by the grace in Jesus Christ. And those things you have heard me teach in public, teach them to trustworthy people who will be competent to teach others. Endure hardship with us like a good soldier of Jesus Christ. No one who serves as a soldier involves himself with everyday concerns. He **is too busy** wanting to please his enlisting officer. Equally, the wrestler never wins the crown unless he wrestles according to the rules.

Also, it's the working farmer who has the first claim on a share of the harvest. Consider what I say for the Lord will give you an understanding of all these things **I tell you.**[1]

Remember Jesus Christ, who was raised from the dead being a descendant of David's. This is my good news for which I am suffering to the point of being in chains like criminals, but the word of God **in me** is not in chains. Therefore, I endure all things for the sake of the elected ones – **those who believe through God's grace** – so that they may receive salvation through Jesus Christ with everlasting glory. The word is faithful and true,

If we died with him, so too shall we live with him
If we endure, so too will we reign with **him**

---

[1] What is the message for Timothy? 1. To focus on pleasing Paul; 2. To follow his instruction; 3. To expect the first share of the rewards for working for Christ.°

If we deny him, so will he deny us
If we cease to believe, he remains faithful
For he cannot deny himself.

Remind them of these teachings. Act as witness to them before God. Do not quarrel for it achieves nothing beneficial but only causes the ruination of those who listen. Do your best to prove yourself before God as a proud labourer who cuts straight through to the true teaching. But avoid profane[1] and empty utterances because they lead to greater impiety. Such words, their talk will spread like gangrene look at Hymenaeus and Philetus who have missed the truth by saying that the resurrection has already taken place and so undermine the faith of some people.[2] However, God's foundations remain firm, **and it is according to our teachings**, having their **double** inscription, "The Lord knows those who are his" and, "Let everyone who calls on the name of the Lord turn away from iniquity." In a stately home there are not only vessels of gold and silver but also of wood and clay; the former are valued and the latter despised. If anyone cleanses himself from these **errors of which I have spoken** he will be, **like the gold and silver ones,** a vessel to be honoured, having been made special and suitable for the master's use and ready to fulfil his good purpose.

Flee from the passions of youth, and pursue righteousness, faith, love and peace together with those who call on the Lord with a pure heart. But refuse to engage in foolish and ignorant questionings **of the faith** in the knowledge that all they achieve

---

[1] Profane is used not to mean "foul language" but more as secular and worldly talk, perhaps philosophical arguments.

[2] This requires explanation. No Christian questioned that the resurrection of Jesus had taken place. What was at issue was whether there would be a resurrection of the dead, in keeping with the belief of the Pharisees, on the Day of Judgement when Jesus would usher in the Kingdom of God. Paul believed in this resurrection of the dead but hedges on the nature of the physical form individuals would have. Hymenaetus and Philetus believed that the resurrection was spiritual and probably took place with the baptism in Christ. This controversy carries on to this very day, when even the physical resurrection of Jesus is perceived by some to be an allegory. The concept of the general physical resurrection of the dead seems to have disappeared as an item of Christian faith.

is quarrelling. It is not appropriate for a servant of the Lord to be aggressive but to be gentle towards all men – teaching with patience and with humility instructing those who disagree. Perhaps, God will cause in them a change of mind to a full knowledge of the truth, so that they come to their senses, having escaped the snare of the devil who had entrapped them to do his will.

You should know this: in the last days times will be difficult. There will be men who love only themselves, who are lovers of money, boasters, arrogant, blasphemers, disobedient to their parents, ungrateful, profane, without affection **for anyone,** unforgiving, slanderers, with no self control, no discipline, who hate the good, who are treacherous, reckless conceited, thrill seekers rather than lovers of God, with the appearance of believing but in reality denying its power. Turn away from them!

They are the types that creep into houses and captivate silly women who overwhelmed by **the guilt for** their sins but tempted by all kinds of wicked desires – always wanting to learn **what to do** but never able to understand the knowledge of the truth. Just as Jannes and Jambres[1] opposed Moses, so do these men oppose the truth – of corrupt mind and counterfeit faith. They will make no progress, for as with the two men **who confronted** Moses, they will make no progress as their folly will become clear to everyone.

But you have closely followed my teaching and my practices – my purpose, faith, patience, love and perseverance, and the persecutions and sufferings which I endured in Antioch, in Iconium and in Lystra; the persecutions I bore and from which the Lord delivered me. And indeed, all those who wish to live piously in Christ will be persecuted, while evil men and impostors will go from bad to worse, deceiving and being deceived. But, you, persevere in what you have learnt, how from infancy you knew the sacred letters of the Scriptures which instructed you for salvation through faith in Jesus Christ. All the holy writings inspired by God are beneficial in their teachings, for the reproof of error, for

[1] The leaders of the Egyptian magicians who challenged Moses when he came before Pharaoh. They are not in the Bible but in Jewish legends.

correcting **people's lives**, for training in righteousness, so that the man of God may be fully equipped for all the good works **required of him.**

Before God and Jesus Christ who will judge the living and the dead, (by his appearing and his Kingdom) as my witnesses, I charge you: proclaim the word, be bold both in favourable or unfavourable times, reprove, admonish and encourage with great patience in teaching it. For the time will come when they will not cope with sensible teachings but to meet their own needs, they will pile up teachers who tickle their ears **by telling them what they want to hear.** They will turn away from hearing the truth in favour of fables. But you must keep your wits about you, endure hardship, do the work of an *evangelist* – the teller of the good news, and fulfil all the obligations of your ministry **to Christ.**

For I am already being poured out as a libation **on God's altar** and the time for departure **of this life** has arrived. I have fought the good fight. I have finished the race. I have kept the faith. Now, the crown of righteousness is stored up for me, which the Lord the righteous judge will award to me and not only to me but to all who have longed for his appearance on that day **of judgement in the kingdom of heaven.**

Come to me as quickly as you can. Demas in his love for worldly things has deserted and gone to Thessalonica. Crescens has gone to Galatia and Titus to Dalmatia. Only Luke[1] is with me. Bring Mark with you for he can be helpful to me in my ministry. I sent Tychicus to Ephesus. Bring with you the cloak I left in Troas with Carpus; also, my scrolls, especially the parchment ones. **I might tell you that** Alexander, the coppersmith behaved very badly towards me. The Lord repay him according to his deeds. You should also be on your guard against him for he is very much opposed to our teachings.

At my first defence, no one was by my side. Everyone deserted me. May it not be counted against them. The Lord, however, stood

---

[1] Some think that is the same Luke who wrote the Gospel and the Acts of the Apostles.

by me and empowered me in order that through me the message would be fully proclaimed so that all the Gentiles would hear it. **Therefore**, I was delivered from the lion's mouth. The Lord will deliver me from every wicked attack and will save me for his heavenly kingdom. To him be glory from age to age. Amen.

Greet Prisca and Aquila and the Onesiphorus household. Erastus remained in Corinth but I left Trophimus ill in Miletus. Hasten to come before winter. Eubulus and Pudens and Linus and Claudia and all the brothers greet you. The Lord be with your spirit. Grace be with you.

APPENDIX 5 · LETTER TO TITUS

FROM: *Paul, a servant of God and an apostle of Jesus Christ, according to the faith of the ones chosen by God and the knowledge of truth that leads to piety – the hope of life eternal which God who does not lie, promised before the beginning of time but fulfilled his word at the appointed time through the teaching entrusted to me by the order of God our Saviour.*
TO: *Titus, my true child who shares our common faith.*
Grace and peace from God the father and our saviour Jesus Christ.

I left you in Crete for this reason to put in order what was left unfinished, to appoint elders in each town as I charged you to do, someone who is blameless, a one-wife husband with believing children who cannot be accused of being uncontrollable and rebellious. It behoves the presiding elder to be irreproachable since he is God's steward, not seeking to please himself alone, not quick to anger, not an alcoholic, not violent, not chasing dishonest gain, but **he should be** hospitable, a lover of that which is good, who is sensible, just, holy, self-controlled; who firmly maintains to the faithful word as it has been properly taught, so that he may encourage others by sensible teachings and be able to refute those who oppose it.

There are many rebellious people, individuals who speak nonsense and deceivers, especially those of the circumcision.[1] It is best to silence them for they are ruining entire households by teaching what is not appropriate – all for the sake of dishonest gain. It was a certain prophet, one of their own countrymen, who said, "Cretans are always liars, wicked brutes and idle gluttons." This testimony is true, so rebuke them severely so that they will be sound in the faith and not pay attention to Jewish myths or to the instructions

---

[1] The Jews who believed in Christ. What follows is an extraordinary blanket attack on Jewish Christians, unless it is an attack on another heresy. In either case it indicates that the author could not have been Paul, who respected different practices within the community and called for harmony and who was not party to the later heresy disputes within the church.

of those who pervert the truth. To the pure all things are pure, but to those who are defiled and unbelieving nothing is pure, but it is their very minds and consciences which are defiled. They profess to know God, but by their works they deny him. They are abominable beings, disobedient and unfit for any good work.

You must teach what is in keeping with sensible teaching: older men should be temperate, serious, sensible, sound in faith, in love and in perseverance; likewise, older women should in their demeanour be reverent, not slanderers, nor given to drinking of too much wine but teachers of what is good in order to train young women to love their husbands and children, to be sensible, pure, good housekeepers, subject to their husbands – otherwise, **if they do not behave this way,** the teachings of God will be maligned.

Also, encourage young men in self-control. In everything set them an example through good works. In your teaching show integrity, seriousness, clean speaking that cannot be criticised so that your opponents will be embarrassed because they will have nothing bad to say about us; slaves – they should be subject to their masters in all matters, trying to please them without contradicting them, without fiddling them, showing that they can be fully trusted. So, will they enhance in all ways the teaching of God our Saviour.

The grace of God that brings salvation has come for all men, which instructs us to reject impiety and worldly desires so that we might live sensibly, righteously and with piety in the present age while we wait for the blessed hope – the glorious appearance of the great God and our Saviour Jesus Christ, who gave himself for us to redeem us from all iniquity and to purify for himself a people to be his own possession, eager to do what is good. These are the things you must speak about – encourage and criticise with all authority. Do not let anyone despise you.

You should remind them to be subject to their rulers and authorities, to be obedient, to be ready to do whatever is good, to rail at no one, to be uncontentious, patient and to be humble with all men. We were once foolish, disobedient, misled, serving **as slaves** all manner of lust and pleasures in a life of wickedness and envy – being hateful and hating one another. But when kindness and the love of man of God our Saviour appeared, he saved us not by **merit of** our righteous deeds but because of his mercy. He saved us through the washing of rebirth and renewal by the divine spirit which he poured out on us to the point of overflowing through Jesus Christ our Saviour, so that having been acquitted by his grace, we might become heirs with the hope of eternal life.

This message is true and reliable. And I want you to affirm with utter confidence so that those who have believed in God should devote themselves assiduously to doing what is good. Doing this is good and profitable for all men. But avoid foolish debates and **contesting** genealogies and quarrels and arguments about the law, for they are futile and without profit. Warn a dissident once and a second time and then avoid him for such a man is perverted and by his sins is self-condemned.

As soon as I send Artemas or Tychicus to you, hasten to come to me in Nicopolis for I have decided to spend the winter there. Do everything for Zenas the lawyer and Apollos when you send them on their way and see that they lack nothing. Also, let our people learn to keep up in the doing of what is good so that they may provide for their needs, lest they lead unproductive lives. Everyone with me sends you greetings. Greet those who love us in the faith. Grace be with all of you.